ENCHANTED RECIPES

Disney

ENCHANTED RECIPES

Thibaud VILLANOVA

Photography: Nicolas LOBBESTAËL
Styling: Soizic CHOMEL DE VARAGNES
Translation: Lisa MOLLE TROYER

INSIGHT 👁 EDITIONS

San Rafael • Los Angeles • London

"THINK
OF THE
HAPPIEST
THINGS, IT'S THE SAME AS HAVING
WINGS... "

PETER PAN (1953)

I could never have guessed that one day, I'd have the privilege of designing recipes from the vast and varied magical kingdom created by Walt Disney!

I've developed recipes for fantasy worlds in the past, but I've never felt the same sense of responsibility I did when crafting recipes from Disney films.

Like many of you, I connected emotionally with Disney's animated films long before I had any real experience of pop culture—certainly before I was aware of it.

As far back as I can remember, my childhood memories are tied to the world of Disney: my first tears of terror while watching *The Black Cauldron*, countless hours spent poring over illustrated storybooks (I still have my copy of *The Great Mouse Detective*), my first trip to the movies with friends from school to see *The Lion King*. In fact, now that I have a son of my own, the only songs I can ever think of when I want to soothe him or make him smile are from *Aladdin* and *Beauty and the Beast*!

Creating something new within the framework of an existing universe is always a challenge: you have to adopt the style and references of the original creators while living up to the expectations of fans who know the imagined world like the back of their hands. In my case, I have to take an idea, a world, or even a subtle reference and transform it into a dish. I did get a little help with the book you're now holding, because every film features a character cooking, serving, or savoring some delicious dish! The food in these films includes the humble feast that Geppetto cooks to celebrate Pinocchio's first day of school; the dishes Lumière describes to Belle in his exuberant song, Abuelita's tamales—which she insists on feeding to Miguel even when he says he's full!—and Little John's stew, so spicy it burns Friar Tuck's mouth. And of course, no Disney cookbook could be complete without Remy, the little chef with the finely honed sense of smell, who concocts a ratatouille that tastes like a symphony in a tribute to classical French cuisine.

I like to say that a well-designed universe gives some thought to its heroes' everyday lives and little pleasures. After all, the characters in these fantasy stories eat just like we do—and like some of us, they can be very fond of their food! The cook in me is delighted to see that Disney has done this with every film since *Snow White and the Seven Dwarfs* was released in 1937.

If you've always wondered how a certain dish in a Disney film tastes, this book is for you. I've poured all my love and enthusiasm into writing the most comprehensive cookbook possible, one that faithfully brings to life the animated films produced by The Walt Disney Studios, from *Snow White and the Seven Dwarfs* to *Wreck-It Ralph*.

I've tried to fill this book with the happiest things by creating colorful recipes and letting the ingredients sing, and by working with my team to stage every recipe in a magical scene.

As Gusteau tells Remy in *Ratatouille*: "Anyone can cook!" I always keep that maxim in mind; it's why I wanted my recipes to be within reach for anyone who wants to cook them. To that end, I've peppered the book with tips and advice between chapters, so that you'll never find yourself lost on this culinary journey through imaginary lands.

On that note, I'll close my introduction. I hope you enjoy reading this book—and cooking from it, of course! Bon appétit!

Thibaud Villanova
Gastronogeek

CONTENTS

THE PRINCESSES

OLD WORLD CUISINE

CONTENTS

GLOBAL CUISINE

WONDERLAND
AND OTHER FANTASY WORLDS

EQUIPMENT

HAND MIXER

BOWL SCRAPER

ROUND COOKIE CUTTER

PARING KNIFE

BLENDER

CHEF'S KNIFE

STEWPOT

MIXING BOWL

WHISK

SAUCEPAN

STAR TIP

LADLE

VEGETABLE PEELER

SILICONE SPATULA

STRAINER

COLANDER

IMMERSION BLENDER

DUTCH OVEN

BUNDT PAN

SPRINGFORM PAN

RAMEKIN

STEAMER BASKET

PASTRY BRUSH

BAKING DISH

PIE PLATE

PIPING BAG

FRYING PAN

RICE COOKER

STAND MIXER

ROLLING PIN

OFFSET SPATULA

WOODEN SPATULA

COOKING THERMOMETER

ZESTER

THE PRINCESSES

BREAKFAST CONGEE

RICE PORRIDGE WITH FRIED EGGS AND BACON

DIFFICULTY:

PREP TIME:
20 minutes

COOK TIME:
50 minutes

INGREDIENTS

YIELD: 1 SERVING

1 stalk lemongrass

1-inch piece ginger

1 clove garlic, in peel

3½ cups Vegetable Stock
(see Tip on page 80 for a homemade stock recipe)

Scant ½ cup (80 g)
short-grain rice

2 tablespoons shelled,
unsalted peanuts

1 large white button
mushroom

A few leaves
flat-leaf parsley

1 thick slice bacon

2 medium eggs

Vegetable oil

Salt and pepper

Congee is a classic Chinese rice porridge. In Mulan, Mushu prepares a special version for the young warrior, which you can make yourself by following this recipe I've created for you.

1. First, prepare the rice porridge and aromatics: Use the flat side of your knife to smash the lemongrass, ginger, and garlic. Place them in a large saucepan and pour in the vegetable stock. Bring to a boil and then add the short-grain rice.

2. Continue to boil over high heat for 3 minutes, stirring often, and then reduce heat to low and simmer for 35 minutes.

3. Meanwhile, crush the peanuts, mince the mushroom, and finely chop the parsley. Set aside.

4. Lay the bacon in a cold frying pan, turn the heat to high, and cook for 3 to 5 minutes, turning regularly. Remove the bacon from the pan and add the peanuts and minced mushroom to the cooking fat. Sauté for 2 minutes and lay on a plate lined with a paper towel to soak up any excess grease.

5. Add a drizzle of vegetable oil to a separate frying pan and warm over high heat. When the oil is hot, crack both eggs into the pan. Lightly season with salt and pepper after the whites have fully cooked. Remove the pan from the heat.

6. Drain the rice. Remove the ginger, garlic, and lemongrass and stir the rice to break it down into a deliciously flavored porridge.

TO PLATE: Pour the congee (porridge) into a large bowl. Arrange the bacon in the shape of a smile. Spread the fried peanut and mushroom mixture over the rice. Sprinkle a few leaves of parsley over top, then arrange the fried eggs to form a face. Enjoy immediately.

NEW WORLD CORN

ROASTED CORN ON THE COB WITH MAPLE SYRUP

DIFFICULTY:

PREP TIME:
10 minutes

COOK TIME:
25 minutes

INGREDIENTS

YIELD: 4 SERVINGS

4 ears fresh corn

8 very thin slices
smoked duck breast
(or bacon)

Maple syrup,
for glazing

This roasted corn recipe pays tribute to the Powhatan people—corn is the golden food that Pocahontas shares with John Smith in the animated film.

1. Preheat the oven to 350°F.

2. Bring a large pot of salted water to a boil. Shuck the corn and boil the ears for 10 minutes.

3. Drain and pat dry. Wrap the base of each ear of corn with slices of smoked duck breast or bacon and then use a pastry brush to coat each ear of corn and the meat with maple syrup.

4. Place the corn directly on the oven rack, with a pan underneath to catch drips, and bake for 15 minutes. Turn the ears regularly and coat with a thin layer of maple syrup every 5 minutes to thoroughly glaze.

5. Serve the corn piping hot and enjoy the balance of sweet and savory flavors!

MOTHER GOTHEL'S SOUP

HAZELNUT PARSNIP SOUP

DIFFICULTY:

PREP TIME:
15 minutes

COOK TIME:
50 minutes

INGREDIENTS

YIELD: 4 SERVINGS

½ cup shelled hazelnuts

2 large parsnips

2 shallots

1 large russet potato

Olive oil

Salt

Pinch of nutmeg

3 cups Vegetable Stock
(see Tip on page 80 for a homemade stock recipe)

Pepper

A few leaves
flat-leaf parsley
for garnishing

Truffle oil

Alone in her secluded tower, Rapunzel sometimes turns to cooking to relieve the boredom, but this hazelnut soup is a special treat that Mother Gothel prepares for her. In the film, we catch a glimpse of parsnips in the witch's basket.

1. Preheat the oven to 350° F.

2. First, prepare the hazelnuts: Spread them out on a baking sheet and toast for 15 minutes in the hot oven, shaking the pan every 5 minutes. Put the toasted hazelnuts on a clean cloth and set aside.

3. Next, make the soup: Peel and dice the parsnips. Peel and finely chop the shallots. Peel the potato and chop into large cubes.

4. Warm a large saucepan over medium heat and then add the olive oil and shallots. Sauté the shallots over medium heat until translucent. Add the chopped vegetables and brown for 3 minutes. Season with salt and a pinch of nutmeg and then pour in the vegetable stock. Bring to a gentle boil and simmer for 25 minutes. When the vegetables are very soft, remove the saucepan from the heat and blend with an immersion blender to achieve a perfectly smooth consistency.

5. Take the hazelnuts and remove their skins: Wrap them into a bundle in the cloth. Holding the bundle tightly closed, rub the hazelnuts together so that the toasted hazelnut skins disintegrate and fall off. After all the skins are removed, crush the hazelnuts and plate the dish.

TO PLATE: Pour the parsnip soup into bowls. Grind fresh black pepper over the soup, add a few drops of truffle oil, and sprinkle with several hazelnut pieces. Finish with a few small leaves of parsley and enjoy!

STROKE OF MIDNIGHT SOUP

CREAM OF PUMPKIN SOUP WITH CHESTNUTS AND ALMONDS

DIFFICULTY:

PREP TIME:
20 minutes

COOK TIME:
45 minutes

INGREDIENTS

YIELD: 4 SERVINGS

1 medium pumpkin

Olive oil

Salt and freshly
ground pepper

Shelled hazelnuts
for garnishing

7 ounces chestnuts,
shelled

3 large russet potatoes

1 leek, white part only

1 large onion

6 cups Vegetable Stock
*(see Tip on page 80 for a
homemade stock recipe)*

1 cup almond milk

½ bunch flat-leaf parsley

*This magical pumpkin soup recipe is a tribute to the fairytale carriage that
brings Cinderella home after the ball!*

1. Preheat the oven to 350°F.

2. First, prepare the pumpkin: Brush it off thoroughly, wash and
   dry. Use a knife to cut off the top of the pumpkin. Remove the
   seeds. With a pastry brush, coat the inside of the pumpkin with
   olive oil. Salt lightly. Repeat the process for the pumpkin top.

3. Place the pumpkin and its top on a baking sheet. Arrange the
   hazelnuts in a single layer on another baking sheet and place
   both sheets in the oven. Toast the hazelnuts for 10 minutes
   and then remove them from the oven. Roast the pumpkin for
   40 minutes, covering with a piece of aluminum foil if it begins to
   get too brown.

4. Meanwhile, prepare the rest of the vegetables and the creamy
   soup base: Bring a large pot of salted water to a boil and cook
   the chestnuts for 15 minutes, until the centers are thoroughly
   cooked.

5. Peel and dice the potatoes. Wash and mince the leek. Peel and
   finely chop the onion.

6. Pour a drizzle of olive oil into a Dutch oven and warm it over
   medium heat. When the oil is hot, add the onion and leek to the
   pan and sauté for 2 minutes. Add the potato and season to taste.
   Cook for 2 minutes to brown the potatoes before pouring in the
   vegetable stock.

7. Put the Dutch oven over high heat until the stock begins to
   boil and then reduce heat to low and simmer for 15 minutes.
   When the vegetables are completely cooked and soft all the
   way through, strain them out, reserving the cooking liquid.
   Drain the chestnuts.

8. Blend the chestnuts and vegetables together. Adjust seasoning. Return the blended vegetables to the cooking pot.

9. Remove the pumpkin from the oven. Use a spoon to gently scoop out the flesh, taking care not to damage the skin, which you will use to serve the soup. Add the roasted pumpkin to the blended vegetables and pour in the almond milk. Use an immersion blender to create a smooth, creamy soup. If the soup is too thick for your taste, thin it with some of the cooking liquid from the vegetables. Check the seasoning and heat the soup to a gentle simmer.

TO PLATE: When the soup is hot, pour it into the pumpkin skin. Finely chop the parsley and sprinkle over the soup. Crush the hazelnuts and invite your guests to garnish their own bowl. Enjoy!

ROYAL SOUFFLÉ

TRADITIONAL CHEESE SOUFFLÉ

DIFFICULTY:

PREP TIME:
20 minutes

COOK TIME:
25 minutes

INGREDIENTS

YIELD: 4 SERVINGS

5 tablespoons butter, divided

Heaping ⅓ cup flour

2 cups milk

5 egg yolks, beaten

Salt

Whole nutmeg

5 ounces fruity Gruyère cheese, grated

8 egg whites

1 tablespoon cornstarch

Beauty and the Beast *is a parade of culinary delights, a few of which even dance past while Lumière sings "Be Our Guest." The menu features beef ragout, pie and pudding "en flambé," and a spectacular cheese soufflé, an iconic dish in classic French cuisine.*

1. Preheat the oven to 350° F.

2. First, prepare a béchamel sauce: Melt 3 tablespoons of butter in a saucepan over medium heat and then add the flour and reduce heat to low to cook for 5 minutes. Gradually pour in the milk while whisking and cook for another 3 minutes, still over low heat. Stirring constantly, add the egg yolks one by one. Add a pinch of salt and freshly grated nutmeg to taste. Mix the grated cheese into the béchamel sauce. Set aside over very low heat.

3. In a small saucepan, melt the remaining butter over very low heat. Use a pastry brush to coat 4 ramekins with melted butter, working from the bottom to the top edge. Place the ramekins in the refrigerator to set the butter. When the ramekins have cooled, brush on more butter and cool again.

4. Add the egg whites and a pinch of salt to a large mixing bowl. Use a hand mixer to whip the egg whites until they form stiff peaks, adding the cornstarch as you go. Stop before the egg whites become too firm. Fold them into the béchamel cheese sauce. Fill the ramekins ¾ full with soufflé batter and bake for 15 minutes.

5. Serve these soufflés to your guests straight from the oven, before they start to deflate!

IMPERIAL JIAOZI

STEAMED DUMPLINGS

Steamed dumplings are a traditional dish in Chinese cuisine. In the film, we see Mulan's father Fa Zhou enjoying them. Now you can make delicious pork dumplings at home!

DIFFICULTY:

PREP TIME:
10 minutes

RESTING TIME:
30 minutes

COOK TIME:
30 minutes

INGREDIENTS

YIELD: 4 SERVINGS

1 carrot

1 clove garlic

1-inch piece fresh ginger

2 ounces bean sprouts

7 ounces shrimp, shelled

7 ounces ground pork

1 egg

1 teaspoon black sesame oil

Salt and pepper

Handful of Thai basil leaves

Handful of cilantro leaves

Olive Oil

Gyoza wrappers

Black vinegar

1. First, prepare the vegetables: Peel and finely grate the carrot. Peel and finely chop the garlic, ginger, and bean sprouts. Coarsely chop the shrimp. Place all the chopped ingredients in a mixing bowl along with the ground pork, egg, and black sesame oil. Salt and pepper lightly and then stir well to evenly mix the filling.

   Finely chop the basil and cilantro and then add them to the filling. Stir again to incorporate the herbs. When your filling is ready, set it aside in the refrigerator.

2. After 30 minutes, bring a large pot of water to a boil and insert a steamer basket coated with a little olive oil to prevent the dumplings from sticking during cooking.

3. Fill the dumplings: Place a gyoza wrapper on your work surface and moisten the outer edge with a little water using a pastry brush. Spoon 1 heaping teaspoon of filling into the center of the wrapper. Fold the wrapper over the filling and press it tightly closed. Repeat until you have used up all the filling. Arrange the dumplings in the steamer basket, cover, and cook for 10 minutes.

TO PLATE: Enjoy these dumplings piping hot with a little black vinegar.

TIANA'S GUMBO

SURF AND TURF GUMBO WITH STEWED OKRA, CHICKEN, AND SHRIMP

DIFFICULTY:

PREP TIME:
20 minutes

COOK TIME:
50 minutes

INGREDIENTS

YIELD: 4 SERVINGS

2 yellow onions

2 cloves garlic

4 shallots

1 stalk celery

1 small green pepper

1 small red pepper

1 medium sweet potato

20 okra pods

2 tablespoons olive oil

Salt and pepper

7 ounces chicken breast

5 ounces precooked smoked
sausage (or andouille)

3 teaspoons Cajun spice
blend, divided

1 tablespoon butter

1 tablespoon flour

8 cups Vegetable Stock
(see Tip on page 81)

2 bay leaves

2 tablespoons flat-leaf parsley,
finely chopped, divided

7 ounces uncooked
shrimp, shelled

Precooked long-grain
rice for serving

Gumbo, a classic Louisiana dish, warms the heart and brings people of all stripes together.

1. First, prepare the aromatics: Peel and finely chop the onions, garlic, and shallots. Rinse and dice the celery. Rinse and deseed the peppers and then dice them as well. Peel the sweet potato and chop into ½-inch cubes. Rinse the okra pods and cut them in half lengthwise.

2. Heat a stewpot over medium heat and pour in the olive oil. When the oil is heated, reduce heat to medium, add all the vegetables except the okra, season lightly, and sauté for 5 minutes until well browned.

3. Meanwhile, prepare the meat: Thinly slice the chicken breast and cut the sausage into ½-inch thick slices.

4. Remove the browned vegetables from the stewpot; then increase the heat slightly and add the chicken strips and slices of sausage. Season with salt and pepper and sprinkle in 1 teaspoon of Cajun spice blend. Sauté the chicken and sausages on all sides to brown and then remove from the stewpot. Make a spicy roux with the pan juices: Melt the butter in the stewpot; then add the flour and 1 teaspoon Cajun spice blend. Stir well and continue to cook over medium to low heat until the roux starts to bubble. Pour in the warm stock while stirring constantly and then return the meat to the stewpot.

5. Add the vegetables, okra, bay leaves, 1 tablespoon of finely chopped parsley, and the remaining Cajun spice blend to the broth. Cover and simmer gently for 30 minutes, stirring often. Remove the pot from the heat and let the gumbo stew and thicken for an additional 10 minutes before dropping in the shrimp, which will be poached and perfectly cooked in the broth. Your gumbo is ready!
   Serve this rich, flavorful gumbo with a generous helping of long-grain rice, sprinkled with the remaining chopped parsley.

TROPICAL KALUA PIG

KALUA PIG WITH POLYNESIAN SAUCE AND CARAMELIZED PINEAPPLE

DIFFICULTY: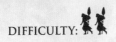

PREP TIME:
20 minutes

COOK TIME:
8 hours

INGREDIENTS

YIELD: 4 SERVINGS

PORK
2¼ pounds boneless
pork shoulder

⅓ cup Alaea red salt
(see Glossary page 47)

3 tablespoons liquid smoke
(see Glossary page 47)

½ fresh pineapple

POLYNESIAN SAUCE
3 tablespoons soy sauce

6 tablespoons rice vinegar

3 tablespoons cooking sake

6 tablespoons pineapple juice

Juice of 1 lime

1 tablespoon ketchup

1 teaspoon cornstarch

CARAMELIZED
PINEAPPLE
½ tablespoons butter

½ fresh pineapple

1 tablespoon brown sugar

1 cup steamed rice

Kalua pig is a traditional Polynesian dish served with fruit and rice—making it is a labor of love. In the film, one of the villagers in Motunui thanks Moana for fixing his roof with a bowl of kalua pig. Now you can make your own succulent island pork!

1. Preheat the oven to 175° F.

2. First, prepare the pork: Slash the meat all over. Sprinkle with red salt and massage it in thoroughly. Repeat the process with the liquid smoke. Set the pork aside.

3. Peel and remove the eyes from half of the pineapple (you will prepare the other half later). Slice the fruit thinly and arrange the slices in a baking dish. Set the seasoned pork shoulder on top. Cover the dish with a sheet of aluminum foil, sealing it completely around the edges, and roast for at least 7½ hours.

4. When the pork is done, remove it from the oven. Pour off the cooking juices and use 2 forks to shred the meat, which should now be tender and fragrant. Set aside.

5. Make the sauce: Pour the soy sauce, rice vinegar, cooking sake, pineapple juice, lime juice, ketchup, and cornstarch into a saucepan and stir well. Cook over medium heat for about 20 minutes to reduce, stirring regularly. Adjust the cooking temperature as needed to keep the sauce from sticking.

6. Clean the second half of the pineapple and dice the fruit. Melt the butter in a small frying pan and add the pineapple pieces. Sprinkle with sugar and brown for 2 minutes over medium heat. When the sugar begins to caramelize, take the pineapple out of the pan and set aside.

TO PLATE: Serve the pulled pork on a plate with steamed rice and some of the browned pineapple. Sprinkle fresh cilantro leaves onto the dish and drizzle sauce over everything. *Keu a ka'ono*!

BEAR CUB BUNS

SCOTTISH SWEET BUNS

This recipe shows you how to make the Scottish sweet buns that Merida's little brothers are so fond of.

DIFFICULTY:

PREP TIME:
15 minutes

COOK TIME:
20 minutes

RESTING TIME: 2 hours

INGREDIENTS

YIELD: 10 SWEET BUNS

BUNS
1 cup cake flour,
plus more for dusting

2 tablespoons
granulated sugar

1 teaspoon vanilla extract

1 teaspoon active dry yeast

1 whole egg plus 4 yolks,
divided

Pinch of salt

⅓ cup butter, softened

ROYAL ICING
1⅔ cup powdered sugar

1 egg white

Juice of ½ orange

10 maraschino cherries
for garnishing

EQUIPMENT
Stand mixer

1. First, prepare the buns: Add the flour, sugar, vanilla, yeast, whole egg, and 3 egg yolks to the bowl of a stand mixer. Add the pinch of salt and then set to medium and mix steadily for 5 minutes. Add the butter and mix for another 10 minutes.

2. Lightly dust a mixing bowl with flour and set the dough in the bowl. Cover with a sheet of plastic wrap and let rise for 1 hour.

3. Take the dough out of the bowl and knead it; then cover again and refrigerate for at least 1 hour.

4. Remove the dough from the refrigerator and allow it to come back to room temperature. Punch the dough down to deflate and then cut into 10 balls of equal size. Preheat the oven to 350° F.

5. Shape the dough balls into buns and space them out on a parchment-lined baking sheet. Stir together the remaining egg yolk with a splash of water and use a pastry brush to lightly coat the tops of the sweet buns. Bake for 12 minutes and then remove the buns from the oven. Let cool completely before icing.

6. While the buns are baking, prepare the royal icing: Put the powdered sugar in a mixing bowl. Add the egg white and stir to completely combine. Pour in the orange juice and continue stirring until the icing is smooth and glossy: Your royal icing is ready. Dip each bun in the icing and top with a maraschino cherry.

Enjoy!

MODERN FAIRY CAKE

TEA-INFUSED BLUEBERRY BIRTHDAY CAKE

DIFFICULTY:

PREP TIME:
1 hour

COOK TIME:
45 minutes

INGREDIENTS

YIELD: 20 SERVINGS
CAKE LAYERS
3½ tablespoons butter

7 whole eggs

2 pinches salt

1 cup granulated sugar

1½ cup flour

vanilla extract

TEA SYRUP
2 cups water

1 cup sugar

Handful of
loose leaf
jasmine tea

If there's one moment in Sleeping Beauty *that makes my mouth water, it's when the good fairies bake a birthday cake for Aurora in their little cottage in the forest. Here's how you can bake your own, no magic wand required!*

1. Preheat the oven to 350°F and put a mixing bowl in the refrigerator.

2. Grease the three springform pans and then prepare the cake batter. In a saucepan, melt the butter over low heat and set aside. Separate the egg yolks and whites in two large mixing bowls. Sprinkle the whites with a pinch of salt and beat until they form stiff peaks; then set aside.

3. Pour the sugar into the mixing bowl with the egg yolks and whisk together until thick and lighter in color. Incorporate the vanilla extract and set aside. Sift the flour and add it gradually to the egg yolk mixture. Fold in the stiff egg whites little by little to obtain a smooth, creamy texture. Finally, stir in the melted butter. Pour the batter into the cake pans and bake for 30 minutes; then remove the cakes from the pans to cool on a wire rack.

4. While the cakes are cooling, make the filling. Prepare a tea-infused syrup: Pour the sugar and water into a saucepan with the loose leaf tea. Heat until the sugar is melted and the water just starts to boil; then remove the saucepan from the heat and let the tea steep in the cooling syrup. Set aside.

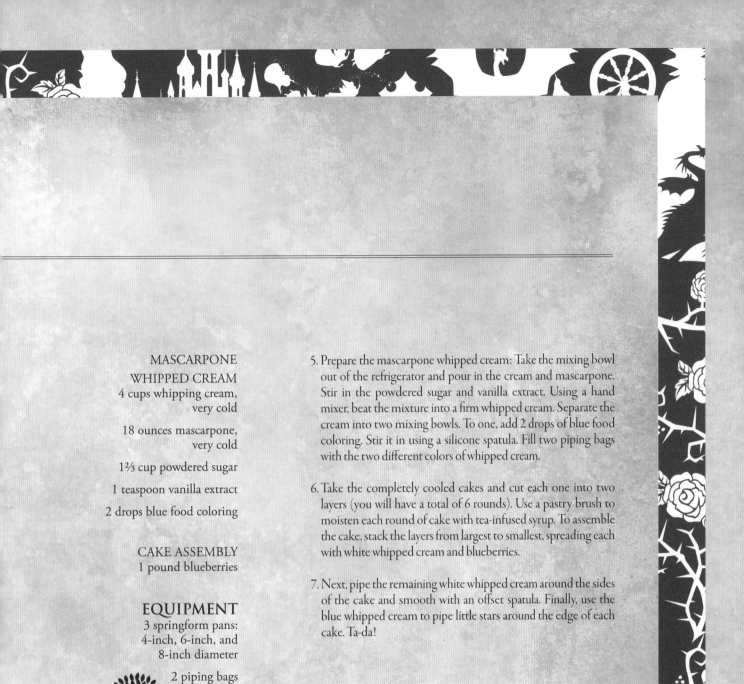

MASCARPONE WHIPPED CREAM

4 cups whipping cream, very cold

18 ounces mascarpone, very cold

1⅔ cup powdered sugar

1 teaspoon vanilla extract

2 drops blue food coloring

CAKE ASSEMBLY

1 pound blueberries

EQUIPMENT

3 springform pans: 4-inch, 6-inch, and 8-inch diameter

2 piping bags

5. Prepare the mascarpone whipped cream: Take the mixing bowl out of the refrigerator and pour in the cream and mascarpone. Stir in the powdered sugar and vanilla extract. Using a hand mixer, beat the mixture into a firm whipped cream. Separate the cream into two mixing bowls. To one, add 2 drops of blue food coloring. Stir it in using a silicone spatula. Fill two piping bags with the two different colors of whipped cream.

6. Take the completely cooled cakes and cut each one into two layers (you will have a total of 6 rounds). Use a pastry brush to moisten each round of cake with tea-infused syrup. To assemble the cake, stack the layers from largest to smallest, spreading each with white whipped cream and blueberries.

7. Next, pipe the remaining white whipped cream around the sides of the cake and smooth with an offset spatula. Finally, use the blue whipped cream to pipe little stars around the edge of each cake. Ta-da!

ARIEL'S MILKSHAKE

PISTACHIO MILKSHAKE WITH STRAWBERRY WHIPPED CREAM

DIFFICULTY: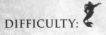

PREP TIME:
15 minutes

INGREDIENTS

YIELD: 4 MILKSHAKES
STRAWBERRY
WHIPPED CREAM
2 cups whipping cream,
very cold

2 tablespoons
mascarpone, very cold

2 tablespoons
Homemade
Strawberry Syrup
(see Tip on page 112)

1 drop red
food coloring

MILKSHAKE
3 cups whole milk

1 cup vanilla
ice cream

2 cups pistachio
ice cream

1 tablespoon
spirulina powder

EQUIPMENT
Piping bag with star tip

Blender

This sweet treat will have you wanting to live under the sea with the mermaids!

1. First, prepare the strawberry whipped cream: Pour the whipping cream and mascarpone into the bowl of a stand mixer and whisk on high speed for 2 minutes. While continuing to whisk, drizzle in the strawberry syrup and food coloring. When the whipped cream is firm and bright red, put it into a piping bag fitted with a star tip. Set aside briefly in the refrigerator.

2. Next, make the milkshake: Add the milk, vanilla and pistachio ice creams, and spirulina powder to a blender and blend on high speed for 2 minutes.

TO SERVE: Pour the milkshake into four large glasses and top each with a generous portion of strawberry whipped cream.

A PIE FOR GRUMPY

CARAMELIZED PLUM PIE WITH VANILLA

DIFFICULTY: 🍎

PREP TIME:
20 minutes

RESTING TIME:
30 minutes

COOK TIME:
30 minutes

INGREDIENTS

YIELD: 4 SERVINGS
SWEET ALMOND
DOUGH

3¼ cups flour

½ cup sugar

¾ cup almond flour

2 whole eggs

¾ cup plus 2 tablespoons
unsalted butter,
at room temperature

PLUM FILLING
3 tablespoons
unsalted butter

28 ounces plums, pitted

½ cup sugar

1 vanilla bean

1 egg yolk

3 tablespoons water

When Snow White asks to stay with the dwarfs, she offers to make them plum pudding and gooseberry pie. Because plums are easier to find, I've used them for the pie she bakes with some help from her woodland friends.

1. First, make the pie crust: Add the flour, sugar, and almond flour to a mixing bowl and stir to combine. In a separate bowl, beat the eggs. Cut the butter into cubes.

2. Rub the butter into the dry mixture with your fingertips until a sandy consistency forms. Add the beaten eggs and knead until the dough forms a smooth ball. Cover tightly with plastic wrap and refrigerate for at least 30 minutes.

3. Meanwhile, prepare the plum filling: Warm a frying pan over medium heat and melt the butter. Add the plums to the hot pan and sauté them in the butter, using a spatula to stir. Add the sugar and stir to combine. Cut the vanilla bean in half and scrape out the seeds into the pan with the plums. Stir again and then cover the pan and stew the fruit for 10 minutes.

4. Preheat the oven to 350°F.

5. Grease a pie plate. Remove the dough from the refrigerator, separate into two parts, and roll each out to form a crust. Use one to line the pie plate and fill it with stewed plums. Cover the filling with the top crust and pinch all around the edges to seal. Trim off any excess dough and shape it into a long ribbon, which you can use to write "Grumpy" on the pie.

6. Beat the remaining egg yolk and mix it with the water. Brush the surface of the pie with the egg wash. Cut a vent into the top of the pie to allow steam to escape. Bake for 30 minutes and serve warm.

SUGAR MILL BEIGNETS

NEW ORLEANS-STYLE BEIGNETS WITH POWDERED SUGAR

DIFFICULTY:

PREP TIME:
20 minutes

RESTING TIME:
2 hours

COOK TIME:
4 minutes

INGREDIENTS

YIELD: 12 SERVINGS
3 tablespoons warm
water (between 100°F
and 110°F)

1 packet (0.75 ounces)
active dry yeast

1⅔ cup flour, divided

⅔ cup whole milk

1 egg

2 heaping tablespoons
sugar

1 teaspoon salt

6 tablespoons butter,
melted

2 cups oil for frying

Powdered sugar
for dusting

EQUIPMENT
Stand mixer

Beignets dusted with powdered sugar are an iconic New Orleans pastry and one of the specialties Tiana serves at the diner where she works. Let me teach you how to make them, too!

1. First, proof the yeast: Pour the warm water into a glass and add the yeast. Leave it for about 10 minutes, until slightly foamy.

2. Attach a dough hook to your stand mixer. Add half the flour, the milk, and the glass of activated yeast to the mixer bowl along with the egg, salt, and sugar. Knead for 30 seconds on slow and then another 2 minutes at medium speed. Add the melted butter and knead for another 2 to 3 minutes. When your beignet dough detaches from the bowl and begins to climb the dough hook, it is finished.

3. Lightly dust your work surface with flour and use a bowl scraper to turn out the dough onto it. Form the dough into a ball and place it in a mixing bowl. Cover with a sheet of plastic wrap and set aside for 1 hour 45 minutes at room temperature.

4. After the dough has doubled in volume, turn it out onto a floured work surface. Punch the dough down to deflate it slightly. Use a rolling pin to roll out the dough and cut it into 10 square or rectangular pieces.

5. In a high-sided pot or deep fryer, heat the frying oil to 370°F (use a cooking thermometer to check the temperature). Drop the beignets into the oil bath and fry for 1 minute 30 seconds on each side, continually pouring hot oil over them with a soup spoon; they should puff up while cooking. When the beignets are golden brown in color, scoop them out of the oil and set immediately on paper towels to drain.

6. Serve the beignets warm, with a generous dusting of powdered sugar.

GLOSSARY OF COOKING TERMS

AGAR-AGAR
Natural gelling product used when preparing jellies, jams, fruit purées, and fondants.

ALAEA RED SALT
Red salt from Hawaii adds a unique flavor and mineral accent to food. Its red color comes from purified volcanic clay.

BEAT
Vigorously whisk a preparation to thoroughly mix ingredients or increase volume.

BLANCH
Technique used to soften an ingredient or reduce its bitterness by dropping it briefly into boiling water and then plunging it into an ice water bath to stop the cooking process. Can also be used to remove the skins of almonds, hazelnuts, pistachios, and tomatoes more easily.

BROWN
Cook meat, fruits, or vegetables in fat either until the juices just begin to caramelize or until the ingredients are fully cooked.

CANDY
Infuse fruit in a sugar syrup to preserve it or make candied fruit.

CRUSH
Smash or cut fruits, vegetables, nuts, or chocolate into uneven pieces.

DOUBLE BOILER
Cooking technique that consists of warming a container by placing it over boiling water.

DICE
Cut vegetables into ⅛-inch cubes.

FINELY CHOP
Use a knife to cut vegetables or herbs into small pieces or thin strips.

FLAMBÉ
Pour alcohol over a dessert, sauce, or fruit and then light it on fire.

GREASE
Coat a pan or dish, usually with butter or oil, to prevent food from sticking.

KNEAD
Make dough by mixing together and working a mixture of ingredients.

LIQUID SMOKE
Liquid smoke is used to add a smoked flavor to your dishes. It is made by condensing the smoke from burning wood.

MARINADE
A seasoned liquid used to flavor meat, fish, or vegetables.

MIXING BOWL
Large, round-bottomed bowl usually made of stainless steel.

MOISTEN
Allow liquid to soak into a cake or cookie to soften or flavor it.

PANKO BREADCRUMBS
Panko breadcrumbs are used in Japanese cooking. These crunchy flakes of toasted bread create a unique crispy feel when used to coat fried foods. You can find them in the international foods aisle or shelved with the traditional breadcrumbs in most well-stocked grocery stores.

PEEL
Remove the skin from a vegetable using a paring knife or vegetable peeler.

PIT
Remove the pits from fruit.

REDUCE
Heat a liquid so that the water in it evaporates, resulting in a thicker consistency and more concentrated flavors.

RESERVE
Keep a mixture or ingredient for later use while preparing a recipe.

RIBBON STAGE
Describes a thick cream or batter that flows slowly off a spoon and stays suspended on the surface for a few moments before gradually disappearing.

SAUTÉ
Use a frying pan to fry ingredients in fat over medium to high heat. The term comes from the French word for jump, because the cook grips the handle of the pan, tilts it so that the ingredients slide down, and then makes them jump back up with a quick flick of the wrist.

SEPARATE AN EGG
Remove the egg yolk from the egg white.

SHAPE
Form dough with your hands.

SIFT
Pass a dry ingredient, such as flour or sugar, through a sieve or sifter to eliminate lumps.

STEW
Slowly cook ingredients in liquid, covered and over low heat, until soft.

THICKEN
Add substance to a liquid, sauce, soup, or cream by adding a binder, such as flour or egg yolk.

TOAST
Brown a dry ingredient, such as coffee beans, almonds, or cloves, without fat to release its flavors.

WELL
A hole made in flour or other dry ingredients to pour the wet ingredients into before mixing.

ZEST
Use a zester or paring knife to remove the zest from a citrus fruit. The zest can be used to add flavor to a cream or other dish.

COLD WORLD
CUISINE

MRS. JUDSON'S CRUMPETS

CHEESE MUFFINS

In The Great Mouse Detective, *Mrs. Judson offers Olivia Flaversham a plate of delicious crumpets when she comes looking for the famous detective. Try baking these savory muffins when you need some comfort food!*

DIFFICULTY:

PREP TIME:
30 minutes

COOK TIME:
35 minutes

INGREDIENTS

YIELD: 8 MUFFINS

⅔ cup milk

⅓ cup plus
1 tablespoon butter

3 eggs

1½ cup flour

2 teaspoons baking
powder

3½ ounces stilton or
cheddar cheese

Pinch of salt

1. Preheat the oven to 350° F.

2. Prepare the batter: First, add the milk and butter to a saucepan. Warm over medium heat until the butter is completely melted. Remove the saucepan from the heat and let cool.

3. Break the eggs into a mixing bowl and whisk vigorously until frothy. Add the milk and butter mixture and stir well to combine.

4. In a separate mixing bowl, stir together the flour and baking powder. Add the egg mixture and stir until the batter is smooth.

5. Grate or crumble the cheese and mix it into the batter. Salt lightly.

6. Pour the batter into 8 lined or greased muffin tins and bake for 15 to 20 minutes.

7. Serve the crumpets warm, with a salad of baby greens.

QUASIMODO'S CROISSANTS

TRADITIONAL PARISIAN CROISSANTS

DIFFICULTY:

PREP TIME:
1 hour

RESTING TIME:
4 hours

COOK TIME:
15 minutes

INGREDIENTS

YIELD: 4 SERVINGS

1 tablespoon
active dry yeast

3 tablespoons
warm water
(between 100° and
110°F)

4 cups cake flour

1 teaspoon table salt

¼ cup sugar

1¼ cups milk

¾ cup plus 1 tablespoon
butter, at room
temperature

1 egg yolk

In The Hunchback of Notre Dame, *the gargoyles tell Quasimodo he's shaped like a croissant is. Here's how to make these iconic French pastries in your own kitchen.*

1. First, mix the yeast into the warm water and leave for 5 minutes to activate.

2. Add the flour, salt, and sugar to a large mixing bowl and stir. Make a well in the center of the dry ingredients and pour the milk in, stirring to incorporate gradually. Then add the water and activated yeast. Stir to combine the ingredients.

3. Dust your work surface with flour and turn the dough out onto it. Knead it with your hands for 12 to 15 minutes and then put the ball of dough back into the mixing bowl and cover. Let rest at room temperature for 2 hours.

4. After the dough has rested, turn it back out onto your lightly floured work surface. Roll it out into a rectangular shape, leaving it a bit thicker in the center. Place the butter in the center of the dough and spread it into an even layer over top, leaving a little space around the edges. Fold the dough in half to enclose the butter. Roll out the dough into a rectangle once again. Fold the dough in thirds like a letter: Fold the bottom ⅓ up, then the top ⅓ down to cover it, and then rotate the rectangle ¼ turn to the right. Roll it out again. Repeat this step 3 times: You've made puff pastry!

5. Now, shape the croissants: roll the puff pastry out thinly into a long rectangle and cut it according to the diagram in the Tips section (see page 82).

6. After you have cut the dough, roll each triangle up, starting with the base and ending with the tip. Curve the ends of the rolled dough together slightly to form a croissant shape. Cover the croissants and let rest for an additional 2 hours.

7. Preheat the oven to 400° F. Beat an egg yolk in a small dish and delicately brush the egg wash over the top of each croissant. Take care not to press down, or you may deflate the pastry. Bake for 15 minutes and enjoy your fresh croissants!

CRÈME DE LA CRÈME À LA EDGAR

CREAM OF JERUSALEM ARTICHOKE WITH NUTMEG

DIFFICULTY:

PREP TIME:
20 minutes

COOK TIME:
1 hour

INGREDIENTS

YIELD: 4 SERVINGS

1 onion

6 Jerusalem artichokes

1 large russet potato

2 tablespoons butter

Salt

Pinch of nutmeg

3 cups chicken stock
*(see Tip on page 82
for Homemade Stock)*

2 cups whipping cream

Homemade Crackers
for serving
(see Tip on page 80)

*In the film, we watch as Edgar prepares a special cream for the cats—
before secretly seasoning it with sedatives. Here's a delicate recipe for
"Crème de la Crème à la Edgar," minus the sedatives, that's designed for
a human palate!*

1. First, prepare the vegetables: Peel and finely chop the onion.
   Peel the Jerusalem artichokes and the potato and then chop
   into cubes.

2. In a large saucepan or Dutch oven, melt the butter over medium
   heat. Add the onion and sauté until translucent. Next, add the
   cubed vegetables and brown for 3 minutes. Season with salt and
   a pinch of nutmeg; then pour in the chicken stock.

3. Bring to a gentle boil and simmer for 20 to 25 minutes. When
   the vegetables are very soft, remove the saucepan from the heat
   and blend with an immersion blender to achieve a perfectly
   smooth consistency.

4. Pour in the cream, stir to fully combine, and adjust seasoning.
   Finally, return the pot to the stove over medium heat and warm
   the soup, stirring regularly. Serve hot.

TO PLATE: Pour the crème de la crème into bowls and serve with
cheese or herb crackers.

REMY'S SOUP

POTATO LEEK SOUP WITH BOURSIN®

DIFFICULTY: ⚲

PREP TIME:
20 minutes

COOK TIME:
35 minutes

INGREDIENTS

YIELD: 4 SERVINGS

1 large onion

3 leeks, white part only

5 russet potatoes

1 stalk celery

Salt and pepper

3 tablespoons butter or
2 tablespoons olive oil

4 cups chicken stock
*(see Tip on page 82 for
Homemade Stock)*

1¾ ounces Garlic & Fine
Herbs Boursin®

Flat-leaf parsley
for garnishing

Ratatouille is a film tribute to classic French cuisine and the art of cooking. Follow this recipe to reproduce the creamy, flavorful soup that Remy makes when he first meets Linguini.

1. First, prepare the vegetables: Peel and thinly slice the onion. Rinse the leeks and slice into rounds. Peel the potatoes and cut into ½-inch cubes. Wash and dice the celery.

2. In a Dutch oven, melt the butter or warm the olive oil over medium heat; then add the onion and sauté for 2 minutes until translucent. Add the leek and celery and season lightly. Sauté for 5 minutes and then add the potatoes and brown for 2 minutes. Pour in the chicken stock. Bring to a gentle boil and simmer, covered, for 25 minutes.

3. When the vegetables are very soft, blend with an immersion blender until smooth. Add the Boursin® and blend for 20 seconds to incorporate. Season to taste.

TO PLATE: Serve this soup piping hot. Just before bringing it to the table, sprinkle a few leaves of parsley over each bowl.

NOSTALGIC RATATOUILLE

MICHEL GUÉRARD'S CONFIT BYALDI

DIFFICULTY: 🗼🗼

PREP TIME:
30 minutes

COOK TIME:
2 hours

INGREDIENTS

YIELD: 4 SERVINGS

COULIS
2 paste tomatoes

3 roasted red peppers
(see Tip on page 112)

1 large white onion

2 cloves garlic

3 cups Vegetable Stock
(see Tip on page 80)

1 teaspoon dried thyme

1 teaspoon dried oregano

Olive oil

Pinch of salt

Ratatouille is a traditional dish from the south of France. When Remy prepares it in the film, it rekindles the childhood memories of food critic Anton Ego. Here's how to make it the right way at home!

1. First, make the coulis. Blanch the tomatoes: Prepare a large bowl of ice water and bring a large pot of water to a boil. Cut an X into the base of each tomato and drop into the boiling water for 30 seconds and then immediately into the ice water bath. Peel the tomatoes and place them in a blender.

2. Add the roasted peppers. Peel and quarter the onion and peel the garlic and then add both to the blender. Add the vegetable stock, thyme, and oregano. Drizzle generously with olive oil and sprinkle with a large pinch of salt. Blend on high for 2 minutes to obtain a fragrant coulis of summer vegetables. Set aside.

3. Preheat the oven to 350°F.

4. Prepare the vegetables for your confit: Wash the zucchinis, eggplants, and tomatoes and use a mandoline or chef's knife to slice them into very thin rounds.

CONFIT

2 yellow zucchini

1 green zucchini

1 eggplant

2 tomatoes

1 graffiti eggplant

½ bunch flat-leaf parsley

A few sprigs rosemary

4 chives

Olive oil

Salt and pepper

5. Pour the coulis into a baking dish in an even layer.

6. Alternating ingredients, lay the vegetable rounds on top of the coulis. Salt and pepper lightly and sprinkle with a few leaves of parsley and the rosemary. Add a thin drizzle of olive oil. Cover the vegetables with a sheet of parchment paper and bake for 1 hour 30 minutes.

TO PLATE: Place a round cookie cutter in the center of your first serving plate. Carefully scoop a portion of vegetable rounds into the cookie cutter. Place a second spoonful of vegetables on top of the first portion. Delicately remove the cookie cutter and place a single chive across the top of the ratatouille. Repeat for each plate. Garnish the plates with a thin line of roasted vegetable coulis and another of olive oil for sauce.

GEPPETTO'S GRILLED FISH

WHOLE GRILLED FISH WITH HERBS AND RUSTIC VEGETABLE HASH

DIFFICULTY:

PREP TIME:
20 minutes

COOK TIME:
35 minutes

INGREDIENTS

YIELD: 4 SERVINGS

2 zucchini

1 eggplant

1 small red pepper

1 small green pepper

4 waxy potatoes

2 onions

4 cloves garlic, divided

Olive oil

2 ounces green olives, pitted

Salt and freshly ground pepper

4 sprigs thyme, divided

2 whole white fish (such as sea bass, snapper, or branzino), scaled and gutted

4 sprigs rosemary

2 sprigs sage

3 tablespoons Compound Butter (see Tip on page 80)

½ lemon

Bursting with pride in his wooden boy, Geppetto decides to prepare a feast to celebrate Pinocchio's first day of school. Here is the recipe for the delicious grilled fish and vegetables that the old man cooks.

1. Preheat the oven to 400°F.

2. First, prepare the vegetables: Wash and rinse the zucchini, eggplant, peppers, and potatoes. Destem and deseed the peppers. Peel the onions. Thinly slice the zucchini, the eggplant, and one onion. Finely chop the other onion, and dice the potatoes and peppers. Smash 2 garlic cloves with the flat side of your knife.

3. Your vegetables are ready to cook. Pour a drizzle of olive oil into a pan and warm it over high heat. When the oil is hot, add the chopped onion to the pan and reduce heat to medium. Sauté for 2 minutes before adding the diced vegetables, smashed garlic, and olives. Stir the vegetables well with a wooden spatula. Salt and pepper, add 2 sprigs of thyme, and cover. Cook for 10 minutes, stirring often.

4. Meanwhile, arrange the slices of zucchini, eggplant, and onion on a baking sheet lined with parchment paper. Using a pastry brush, lightly coat the vegetables with olive oil. Salt and pepper lightly and bake for 10 minutes.

5. Prepare the fish: Using a sharp knife, carefully make diagonal cuts into the fish, making sure not to cut too deeply. Smash the remaining 2 garlic cloves and place 1 inside the cavity of each fish, along with the rosemary, sage, and remaining thyme. Salt and pepper lightly.

6. Cook the fish using one of the following methods:
– Broil in the oven for 15 minutes, turning the fish over halfway through;
– Brush a grill pan with a thin layer of olive oil. Warm over medium heat and, when the oil is hot, grill the fish for 5 minutes on each side.

TO PLATE: Spread the sautéed vegetable hash out on a serving plate. Add the roasted vegetables and arrange the grilled fish on top. Finally, garnish each hot, grilled fish with a bit of compound butter and a lemon slice.

Enjoy!

KAY'S BANQUET

SPICED TURKEY WITH ROASTED VEGETABLES

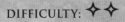

DIFFICULTY: ✦✦

PREP TIME:
30 minutes

COOK TIME:
3 hours

INGREDIENTS

YIELD: 4 SERVINGS

One 8-pound turkey, trussed

SPICED BUTTER AND TURKEY HERBS

¾ cup salted butter

1 teaspoon ground cumin

1 teaspoon ground coriander

1 teaspoon ground ginger

Salt and pepper

1 stick cinnamon

1 bunch fresh flat-leaf parsley

VEGETABLES

3 onions

2 pounds carrots

2 cloves garlic

20 ounces baby potatoes

Sunflower oil for greasing the pan

Salt and pepper

8 cups Chicken or Turkey Stock, divided
(see Tip on page 82)

When Wart is working for Sir Ector, we see Kay and his father sitting at the table, devouring a roast turkey. Now you can feast like a knight!

1. Preheat the oven to 425°F.

2. First, make a spiced butter for your turkey: Put the butter in a mixing bowl and stir with a silicone spatula until softened. Add the cumin, coriander, and ginger. Continue mixing with the spatula to evenly distribute the spices.

3. Lightly salt the cavity of the turkey and place the cinnamon stick and fresh parsley inside. Loosen the turkey skin gently with your fingers, taking care not to tear it, and rub the spiced butter over the flesh. You can use a piping bag to make this step easier.
   When the turkey is well coated with butter, set it aside.

4. Next, prepare your vegetables: Peel and thinly slice the onions. Wash the carrots and cut them into thirds, on the diagonal. Smash the garlic. Wash and dry the potatoes.

5. Grease a large baking dish and place all the vegetables in the bottom. Season to taste with salt and pepper. Place the turkey on top of the vegetables and pour a little stock into the dish. Make sure that the stock does not touch the turkey at this point. Roast for 30 minutes, watching the turkey to make sure it doesn't burn.

6. Meanwhile, prepare the glaze for the turkey: Add the honey, cumin, and turmeric to a mixing bowl. Mix well and set aside.

7. After the turkey has roasted for 30 minutes, reduce the oven heat to 300°F. Remove the baking dish from the oven. Stir the vegetables and add more stock to cover.

GLAZE

1¼ cups honey

1 teaspoon ground cumin

2 teaspoons turmeric

8. Drizzle ¼ of the spiced honey over the meat and use a pastry brush to spread it. Bake for 2 hours 30 minutes, removing the turkey from the oven every 50 minutes to glaze it with honey.

9. Thanks to the spiced butter and honey, the meat should be perfectly cooked, juicy, and deliciously spiced. Serve with the roasted vegetables.

LITTLE JOHN'S SPICY STEW

FOUR-HOUR BEEF AND VEGETABLE STEW

DIFFICULTY:

PREP TIME:
30 minutes

COOK TIME:
4 hours

INGREDIENTS

YIELD: 4 SERVINGS

2 large onions

1 clove garlic

½-inch piece fresh ginger

1¾ pounds stew meat or beef cheek

Salt and freshly ground pepper

Handful of flour for dredging the meat

Vegetable oil

3 tablespoons unsalted butter

8 cups dark beer

2 cups Vegetable Stock *(see Tip on page 80)*

2 tablespoons tomato paste

1 bunch flat-leaf parsley

4 carrots

In Robin Hood, Little John seems to be in charge of the cooking. He makes a steaming pot of delicious stew . . . that's a bit too spicy for Friar Tuck's delicate taste buds! Here is a recipe for a traditional English stew just like Robin Hood's sidekick would have made.

1. First, peel and coarsely slice the onions. Use the flat side of your knife blade to smash the garlic and ginger. Set aside.

2. Cut the meat into bite-sized pieces, salt and pepper lightly and then roll each piece in flour.

3. Warm a large Dutch oven over medium heat and add a generous drizzle of vegetable oil. When the pot and oil are hot, add the meat and brown on all sides. The goal is to create a brown crust on the surface of the meat, which will keep it tender during cooking.

4. Remove the meat from the Dutch oven and add the butter. Sauté the onions in the melted butter for 3 to 4 minutes; then add the garlic and ginger and sauté for an additional 2 minutes before deglazing the pot with the beer. Use a wooden spatula to stir the stew and scrape the sucs off the bottom of the pot. Add the stock and tomato paste. Coarsely chop the parsley and add it to the Dutch oven along with the meat. Bring to a gentle boil and simmer for 2 hours.

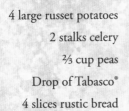

4 large russet potatoes

2 stalks celery

⅔ cup peas

Drop of Tabasco®

4 slices rustic bread

5. Meanwhile, prepare the vegetables: Peel the carrots and potatoes and cut into bite-sized cubes. Dice the celery and rinse the peas.

6. After the meat has cooked for 2 hours, put all the vegetables into the Dutch oven, add a drop of Tabasco®, and simmer over low heat for another 2 hours, stirring frequently and leaving the lid slightly open. When the stew is done cooking, the meat should be meltingly tender.

TO PLATE: Pour the stew into soup bowls and serve with thick slices of toasted rustic bread. Cheers!

TOURNAMENT FRUIT PIE

BLACKBERRY ALMOND PIE

DIFFICULTY:

PREP TIME:
30 minutes

COOK TIME:
35 minutes

INGREDIENTS

YIELD: 4 SERVINGS

6 cups blackberries

½ cup sugar

Scant 3 tablespoons cornstarch

3 tablespoons lemon juice

14 ounces Sweet Almond Dough
(see Tip on page 81)

1 egg yolk

At the archery tournament hosted by Prince John, where Robin Hood competes disguised as a stork, there is a stand selling blackberry pies. Now you can make them yourself!

1. Preheat the oven to 350°F.

2. First, prepare the filling: Wash the blackberries in a thin stream of running water. Place them in a saucepan along with the sugar, cornstarch, and lemon juice. Stir to combine and cook for 20 minutes over medium heat, stirring frequently to prevent the berries from sticking to the pan. Remove the pot from the heat and set aside.

3. Divide the ball of dough in half and use a rolling pin to roll both pieces out on a floured work surface. Line a deep pie dish with the first round of dough and then use a fork to prick the crust all over, including the sides.

4. Pour the blackberry filling into the pie crust and spread it out evenly with the back of a spoon. Cover with the second round of dough and pinch all around the edges to seal. Trim off the excess dough and shape it into decorations for the pie crust. Cut a ½-inch hole in the center of the pie to serve as a vent so that steam can escape during cooking.

5. Beat the egg yolk in a bowl and brush it over the surface of the pie. Bake for 35 minutes.

TO PLATE: This pie is best served warm, in generous slices!

KANINE KRUNCHIES

VANILLA AND CINNAMON BISCUITS

DIFFICULTY:

PREP TIME:
10 minutes

RESTING TIME:
1 hour

COOK TIME:
10 minutes

INGREDIENTS

YIELD: 18 BISCUITS
(FOR HUMANS!)

1½ cups flour

⅓ cup sugar

1 teaspoon
vanilla extract

⅔ cup almond flour

1 teaspoon
ground cinnamon

1 teaspoon ground
ginger

Pinch of salt

½ cup plus
2 tablespoons
unsalted butter

1 egg

In 101 Dalmatians, our canine friends see a television commercial for these delicious cookies. Here's a version that humans will enjoy!

1. Prepare your cookie dough: Sift together the flour, sugar, vanilla extract, almond flour, ground cinnamon, ginger, and salt into a mixing bowl. Stir well.

2. Melt the butter and mix it into the dry ingredients. Add the egg and stir to obtain a smooth dough. Wrap the ball of dough in plastic wrap and refrigerate for 1 hour.

3. Preheat the oven to 325°F.

4. Dust your work surface with flour and roll out the dough to ⅜ inch thick using a rolling pin. Use a bone-shaped cookie cutter to cut the dough into cookies and then place them on a baking sheet lined with parchment paper. Bake for 10 minutes before removing the cookies to a wire rack to fully cool. Kanine Krunchies can't be beat!

TIPS

VEGETABLE STOCK

Prep time: 10 minutes
Cook time: 2 hours
Resting time: 30 minutes

INGREDIENTS
4 carrots, chopped

1 leek, white part only

½ stalk celery

1 onion

1 bouquet garni (green part of 1 leek, 4 stems parsley, 1 stalk fennel, 1 bay leaf, 1 sprig thyme)

1 shallot

8 cups water

⅔ cup white wine

1 star anise

3 cardamom pods

Place the carrots, leek, celery, onion, bouquet garni, shallot, water, white wine, star anise, and cardamom pods in a stewpot and simmer for 2 hours, covered. Remove stock from heat and let cool for 30 minutes, then strain.

COMPOUND BUTTER

Prep time: 10 minutes

INGREDIENTS
½ cup salted butter
¼ bunch fresh flat-leaf parsley
Juice of 1 lemon

Beat the butter in a mixing bowl with a silicone spatula until softened. Set aside.

Wash, dry, and finely chop the parsley and add it to the butter. Add the lemon juice and combine all the ingredients using the silicone spatula.

Wrap the butter in a piece of plastic wrap and store in the refrigerator until you are ready to use it.

CHEESE CRACKERS

Prep time: 10 minutes
Resting time: 1 hour
Cook time: 15 minutes

INGREDIENTS
1 cup plus one tablespoon flour
5 tablespoons salted butter at room temperature
1 egg
2½ ounces roquefort cheese

Add the flour, butter, and egg to a mixing bowl. Knead with your fingertips and work in the roquefort in small chunks. Continue kneading until you have a smooth ball of dough.

Shape the dough into a neat roll and wrap tightly with plastic wrap. Refrigerate for 45 minutes to 1 hour.

Preheat the oven to 350°F.

Take the dough out of the refrigerator and remove the plastic wrap. Slice the dough into thin rounds and arrange them on a baking sheet lined with parchment paper. Bake for 15 minutes and enjoy!

GUMBO STOCK

Prep time: 20 minutes
Cook time: 2 hours
30 minutes

INGREDIENTS
YIELD: 8 CUPS OF STOCK
1 large onion
1 head garlic
2 large carrots
1 stalk celery
½ teaspoon crushed black peppercorns
1 clove
Vegetable oil
Carcass of 1 small chicken
Leftover shrimp shells from Tiana's Gumbo recipe (page 30)
Salt
1 bay leaf
2 sprigs thyme
2 sprigs tarragon
½ bunch flat-leaf parsley
3 stems basil

First, prepare the mirepoix for your stock: Peel the onion, cut the head of garlic in half horizontally, and peel the carrots. Chop the onion and carrots. Rinse and dice the celery. Set aside the mirepoix.

Warm a frying pan over medium heat and toast the black pepper and clove for 2 minutes, dry, then remove from the pan.

Add a drizzle of vegetable oil to a large pot. When the oil is hot, sauté the onions and carrots for 3 minutes, stirring frequently. Add the garlic to brown lightly, taking care not to let it burn. Add the chicken carcass and shrimp shells. Season with a generous pinch of salt and brown for 5 minutes. (Remember to crush the carcass and shells—a rolling pin works well.)

Pour in 10 cups of water and add the bay leaf, thyme, tarragon, parsley, and basil.

Bring to a gentle boil and then cover and simmer over low heat for 2 hours 30 minutes.

SWEET ALMOND DOUGH

Prep time: 10 minutes
Resting time: 30 minutes

INGREDIENTS
3¼ cups flour
½ cup sugar
¾ cup almond flour
2 eggs
¾ cup plus 2 tablespoons unsalted butter at room temperature

Add the flour, sugar, and almond flour to a mixing bowl. In a separate bowl, beat the eggs with a fork. Set aside.

Cut the butter into cubes and add it to the dry ingredients in the mixing bowl. Rub the butter into the flour mixture with your fingertips until it looks sandy. Add the beaten eggs and knead to incorporate.

The dough is ready when it forms a smooth ball in your hands: Cover it tightly with plastic wrap and refrigerate for 30 minutes.

TIPS

HOW TO CUT AND SHAPE CROISSANTS

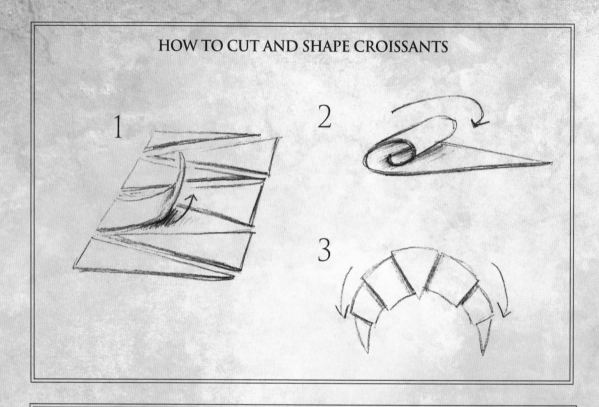

CHICKEN OR TURKEY STOCK

Prep time: 20 minutes
Cook time: 4 hours

INGREDIENTS

4½ pounds chicken or turkey carcass
6 tablespoons grapeseed oil
3 tablespoons unsalted butter
1 clove garlic
2 shallots
1 bouquet garni (thyme and
bay leaf tied in a green leek leaf)
1 sprig rosemary
2 juniper berries
Pinch of crushed peppercorns

Preheat the oven to 300° F.

Crush the turkey or chicken carcass and sauté it in a stewpot with the grapeseed oil and butter. Stir and cook over medium heat until the carcass turns golden brown. Remove it from the pot.

Skim off the fat, but leave the cooking juices in the pot. Simmer the garlic and shallots in the cooking juices for 5 minutes over medium heat. Pour in 8 cups of water, add the bouquet garni, and cook in the oven for 4 hours.

30 minutes before the stock is finished, add the rosemary, juniper berries, and peppercorns to the stewpot; then return it to the oven. These spices will add depth and flavor to your stock.

After 4 hours, strain the contents of the stewpot, saving only the liquid.

HOMEMADE FRIES

IN THE DEEP FRYER

Prep time: 15 minutes
Cook time: 10 minutes

INGREDIENTS
YIELD: 4 SERVINGS
1 large carrot
2 small parsnips
¼ winter squash
4 russet potatoes
Oil for frying
Coarse salt for sprinkling

Peel the carrot, parsnips, winter squash, and potatoes. Cut them into sticks lengthwise. Rinse with cold water and then drain and pat thoroughly dry.

Line a tray with paper towels.

Pour the frying oil into a large pot or deep fryer and heat it to 330°F (use a cooking thermometer to check the temperature). Use a skimmer or frying basket to lower the vegetable sticks into the hot oil. Fry for 5 minutes and then lay the fries on the paper towels for 5 minutes.

Return to the fryer for another 2 minutes.

Spread the fries out on a layer of paper towels and then serve them on a plate while still piping hot. To enhance their flavor, sprinkle with a pinch of coarse salt, for sprinkling!

IN THE OVEN

Prep time: 15 minutes
Cook time: 30 minutes

INGREDIENTS
YIELD: 4 SERVINGS
1 large carrot
1 large sweet potato
1 eggplant
1 zucchini
4 russet potatoes
1 teaspoon dried thyme
1 teaspoon minced garlic
2 teaspoons chopped fresh parsley
Generous pinch of salt
Generous pinch of pepper
⅓ cup olive oil

Peel the carrot, sweet potato, eggplant, zucchini, and russet potatoes. Cut them into sticks lengthwise. Place the vegetable sticks in a large zipper storage bag.

Add the thyme, persillade, salt, pepper, and olive oil. Seal the bag and massage the contents to fully coat the vegetable sticks with the herbs and olive oil.

Preheat the oven to 350°F.

Arrange the vegetable sticks in a single layer on a baking sheet. Sprinkle them lightly with salt and pepper and bake for 30 minutes, turning them over halfway with a pair of tongs. Remove your vegetable fries from the oven and serve hot!

GLOBAL
CUISINE

KRONK'S SPINACH PUFFS

SPINACH AND SHEEP MILK CHEESE TURNOVERS

DIFFICULTY:

PREP TIME:
20 minutes

COOK TIME:
30 minutes

INGREDIENTS

YIELD: 16 TURNOVERS

2 shallots

1 clove garlic

2 pounds fresh spinach

Olive oil

1 egg plus 1 egg yolk, divided

10½ ounces ricotta cheese

3½ ounces Basque sheep's milk cheese or queso manchego, grated

8 sun-dried tomatoes

1 pound puff pastry

Salt and pepper

Kronk is not just Yzma's henchman; he's also a connoisseur of gourmet food. You can make his famous spinach puffs at home by following this recipe!

1. Preheat the oven to 350° F.

2. Prepare the vegetables: Peel and finely chop the shallots. Peel and chop the garlic. Rinse and dry the spinach and then destem and coarsely chop.

3. Pour a drizzle of olive oil into a frying pan and warm it over medium heat. When the pan is very hot, add the shallots and sauté for 2 minutes. Add the garlic and sauté for another 2 minutes, taking care not to let the garlic burn. Add the spinach. Stir well and season lightly with salt and pepper. Cover and reduce heat to low. Cook for 10 minutes to wilt the spinach, stirring frequently with a wooden spatula. Remove pan from heat and set aside.

4. Break the whole egg into a mixing bowl and beat. Add the ricotta and grated cheese and mix. Chop the sun-dried tomatoes and stir them into the mixture, followed by the spinach. The filling is ready.

5. Dust your work surface with flour and roll out the puff pastry. Cut it into 16 rectangles. Scoop a generous spoonful of filling into the center of each pastry rectangle. Moisten the edges, fold over, and seal to form turnovers.

6. Beat the egg yolk with 1 tablespoon of water in a bowl and brush the mixture over each turnover. Bake for 15 minutes. Serve hot.

AUNT CASS'S WINGS

SPICED CHICKEN WINGS

DIFFICULTY:

PREP TIME:
15 minutes

RESTING TIME:
2 hours

COOK TIME:
50 minutes

INGREDIENTS

YIELD: 4 SERVINGS

4 cups buttermilk

20 chicken wings
or drumettes

½ bunch fresh cilantro
for garnishing

Olive oil, for frying

MARINADE

½-inch piece fresh ginger

2 cloves garlic

1 teaspoon
onion powder

1 teaspoon
ground paprika

½ teaspoon
cayenne pepper

1 teaspoon brown sugar

3 tablespoons soy sauce

2 tablespoons rice vinegar

1 tablespoon
cooking sake

2 tablespoons
tomato paste

1 tablespoon sesame oil

In Big Hero 6, *teenager Hiro lives with his Aunt Cass, who owns a café in the city of San Fransokyo. Here is the recipe for one of her signature dishes, her "melt-your-face-off" chicken wings, which she cooks for Hiro.*

1. First, prepare the meat: Pour the buttermilk into a mixing bowl and add the chicken wings. Cover the surface with plastic wrap and refrigerate for at least 1 hour. The buttermilk will soak into the chicken meat and tenderize it. Drain off the buttermilk and put the wings into a freezer bag. Set aside.

2. Now make the spicy marinade: Peel and finely chop the ginger and garlic. Add them to a mixing bowl with the onion powder, paprika, cayenne pepper, brown sugar, soy sauce, rice vinegar, sake, tomato paste, and sesame oil. Stir well to combine into a flavorful liquid. Pour the marinade into the bag with the chicken, seal the bag and then knead the meat to thoroughly coat all the wings. Refrigerate the wings in the marinade for 1 hour before cooking.

3. Preheat the oven to 400° F.

4. Prepare your oven fries: Wash and dry the potatoes. Cut them into fries and add to a mixing bowl along with the olive oil. Salt and pepper lightly and sprinkle with a pinch of ground paprika. Stir to evenly coat the fries with the oil and spices. Spread out the fries in a single layer on a baking sheet lined with parchment paper. Bake for 35 minutes.

5. Meanwhile, remove the bag of chicken wings from the refrigerator. Pour a drizzle of olive oil into a frying pan over high heat and add the wings when the oil is very hot. Fry for 2 minutes on each side and then reduce the heat to low. Cook for another 10 minutes on each side and then remove the wings from the pan.

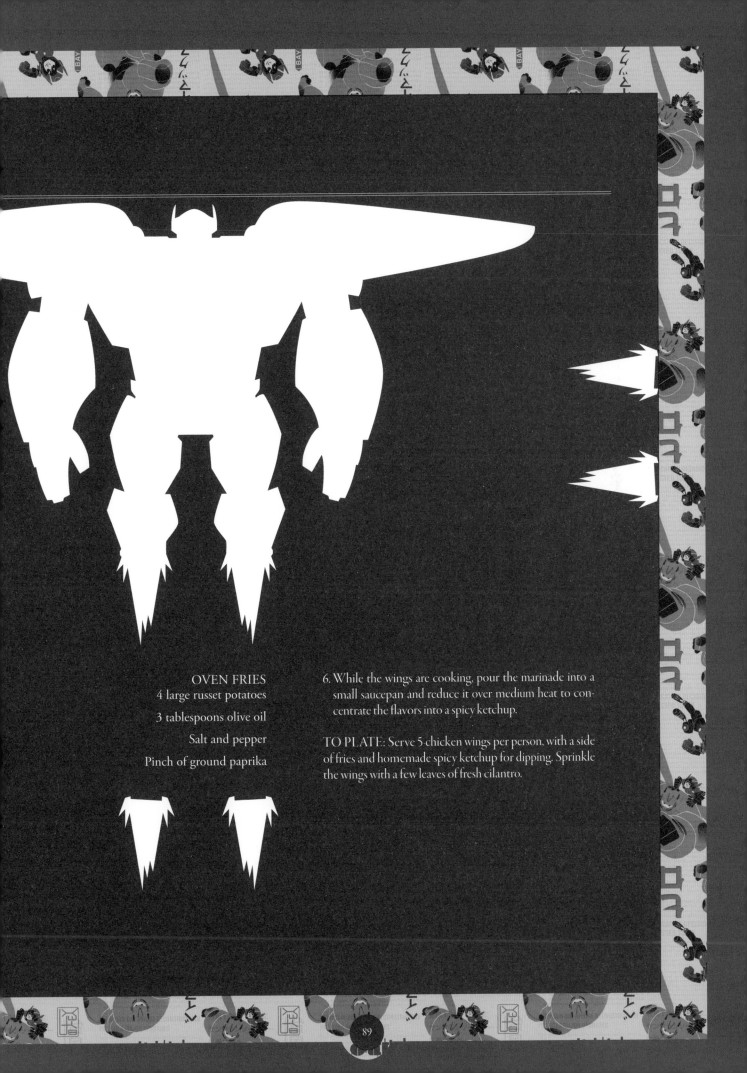

OVEN FRIES
4 large russet potatoes

3 tablespoons olive oil

Salt and pepper

Pinch of ground paprika

6. While the wings are cooking, pour the marinade into a small saucepan and reduce it over medium heat to concentrate the flavors into a spicy ketchup.

TO PLATE: Serve 5 chicken wings per person, with a side of fries and homemade spicy ketchup for dipping. Sprinkle the wings with a few leaves of fresh cilantro.

DATE NIGHT DINNER

ITALIAN SPAGHETTI AND MEATBALLS

DIFFICULTY:

PREP TIME:
20 minutes

COOK TIME:
1 hour 10 minutes

INGREDIENTS

YIELD: 4 SERVINGS

10 ounces spaghetti

A few fresh basil leaves
for garnishing

MEATBALLS

2 tablespoons milk

1 tablespoon fine
breadcrumbs

1 tablespoon
chopped hazelnuts

9 ounces ground beef

7 ounces uncooked
Italian sausage,
removed from casing

1 egg

1 teaspoon dried oregano

1 teaspoon dried thyme

1 teaspoon dried
rosemary

1 teaspoon
onion powder

½ teaspoon salt

Generous pinch
of pepper

Lady and the Tramp features Disney's most iconic romantic dinner, when the two dogs share a plate of spaghetti at Tony's Restaurant. Here's how to cook up your own delicious spaghetti and meatballs.

1. First, make the meatballs: Add the milk, breadcrumbs, and hazelnuts to a mixing bowl. Add the beef, Italian sausage, egg, oregano, thyme, rosemary, onion powder, salt, and pepper. Stir well using a fork. Finely chop the mint leaves and add them to the meat mixture.

2. Lightly dust your hands with flour to prevent sticking, and form the mixture into 2-inch balls. Pour more flour into a dish and roll the meatballs in it to fully coat. Shake off any excess flour.

3. Cook the meatballs: Pour the olive oil into a frying pan and warm it over high heat. When the oil is hot, add the meatballs. Sear them for 40 seconds on each side without turning to form a crust. When the meatballs are nicely browned on the outside, remove from the heat and set aside while you make the sauce.

4. First, prepare the mirepoix: Peel and dice the shallots, onions, and carrot.

5. Pour 2 tablespoons of olive oil into a Dutch oven and warm over medium heat. When the oil is hot, add the shallot, onion, and carrot. Stir well and sauté until the vegetables just begin to brown.

A few fresh mint leaves

2 tablespoons flour,
plus more for coating

1 tablespoon olive oil

PASTA SAUCE

2 shallots

2 onions

1 carrot

2 tablespoons olive oil

2 cloves garlic

½ cup Vegetable Stock
(see Tip on page 80)

4 cups tomato sauce

Salt and pepper

1 teaspoon
granulated sugar

1 tablespoon Italian
herbs

6. Smash the garlic and add it to the pot. Pour in the vegetable stock to deglaze before adding the tomato sauce. Stir again and season with salt and pepper. Add the sugar, and stir and then add the Italian herbs. Drop the meatballs into the sauce. Reduce the heat and cover the Dutch oven, leaving the lid slightly open for steam to escape. Continue cooking over low heat for 1 hour and then reduce heat to its lowest setting while you cook the pasta.

7. Bring a large pot of salted water to a boil and drop in the spaghetti. Follow the directions on the box to cook, then drain the pasta, and immediately dish it into four soup bowls.

8. Divide the meatballs among the bowls and add a generous spoonful of sauce. Garnish with a few fresh basil leaves and enjoy.

Buon appetito!

PIZZA PLANET SUPER NOVA BURGER

VEAL AND BEEF BURGERS WITH AVOCADO AND SPICY MAYONNAISE

DIFFICULTY:

PREP TIME:
20 minutes

RESTING TIME:
30 minutes

COOK TIME:
10 minutes

INGREDIENTS

YIELD: 4 BURGERS

BURGER PATTIES

2 shallots

9 ounces ground veal

5 ounces ground beef

1 egg

1 teaspoon ground cumin

1 teaspoon paprika

1 roasted red pepper
(see Tip on page 112)

Salt and pepper

1 avocado

4 tablespoons butter

BURGER

4 slices cheddar cheese

Spicy Mayonnaise
(see Tip on page 113)

4 hamburger buns,
homemade *(see Tip on
page 113)* or store bought

4 teaspoons caramelized
onion jam

Lettuce leaves for
topping the burgers

In the Toy Story *world, Pizza Planet is a spaceport-themed fast food restaurant and arcade that serves fabulous burgers like the Super Nova. Try one for yourself!*

1. First, prepare the meat for the patties: Peel and finely chop the shallots. Add them to a mixing bowl with both types of ground meat. Add the egg, cumin, and paprika. Mix with a fork to combine all the ingredients.

2. Coarsely chop the roasted pepper and add it to the meat mixture. Salt and pepper lightly; stir again. Pit the avocado, dice the flesh, and delicately fold it into the meat.

3. Cover the meat mixture and refrigerate for 30 minutes; then remove it from the refrigerator, lightly flour your hands, and divide into 4 portions. Form each into a thick patty and set aside on a lightly floured work surface.

4. Heat a frying pan over high heat and cook the burgers: Melt 1 tablespoon of butter per patty and then set each patty in the melted butter. Fry for 30 seconds on each side to form a brown crust and then reduce heat to low to continue cooking for another 4 minutes on each side.

5. After the patties are cooked, set a slice of cheddar on top of each. Cover the pan, remove from the heat, and set aside briefly.

6. Assemble the burgers: Spread spicy mayonnaise onto the hamburger buns. Add some caramelized onion jam, a few lettuce leaves, and a patty with cheese to the base of the bun and then top with the other half of the bun.

TO PLATE: Serve these burgers with Homemade Fries *(see Tip on page 83)* and spicy mayonnaise.

PRINCE ALI'S KEBABS

SUMAC-SPICED LAMB AND GRILLED VEGETABLE SKEWERS

DIFFICULTY:

PREP TIME:
20 minutes

COOK TIME:
10 minutes

INGREDIENTS

YIELD: 4 SERVINGS

2 spring onions

2 cloves garlic

14 ounces ground lamb

7 ounces ground beef

1 teaspoon ground cumin

1 teaspoon ground sumac

Salt and pepper

1 white onion

1 red onion

1 cluster cocktail tomatoes

1 small red pepper

Olive oil

When Prince Ali makes his sensational entrance into Agrabah and the Genie sings about the details of the grand entourage, we see cooks holding out fat skewers of spiced meats. Now you can make these delicious kebabs that are fit for a prince!

1. Peel and finely chop the spring onions (white and green part). Peel and chop the garlic.

2. Add both types of ground meat to a mixing bowl. Add the garlic, onion, cumin, and sumac. Salt and pepper lightly. Use a fork to stir thoroughly until the ingredients are evenly distributed and the mixture is fragrant. Set aside briefly in the refrigerator.

3. Prepare the vegetables for your kebabs: Peel the white and red onions and cut into thick (½-inch) slices. Wash the tomatoes. Wash and deseed the pepper and cut into bite-sized pieces.

4. Take the meat out of the refrigerator and use your fingers to form small meatballs (you can dust your hands with flour first to prevent sticking). Thread the meatballs onto skewers, alternating them with onion slices, pepper pieces, and tomatoes. Lightly brush each kebab with olive oil.

5. Preheat your barbecue grill or a grill pan over high heat. Sear the meatballs on each side before reducing the heat to medium. Cook the skewers for 5 minutes on each side. At the end of cooking, you can squeeze fresh lemon over the meatballs for extra zip.

ABUELITA'S TAMALES

MARINATED CHICKEN TAMALES

In Mexico, family recipes for tamales are passed down from generation to generation. Miguel's grandmother, Abuelita, makes them often, and won't take no for an answer when she offers them to Miguel! Follow along to make Abuelita's tamales at home.

DIFFICULTY:

PREP TIME:
45 minutes

RESTING TIME:
1 hour 20 minutes

COOK TIME:
1 hour 35 minutes

INGREDIENTS

YIELD: 10 TAMALES

14 ounces chicken breast

10 dried corn husks

Salt

Olive oil, for frying

MARINADE

1 very ripe avocado

2 cloves garlic

1 large onion,
peeled and chopped

Juice of 2 limes

⅔ cup pineapple juice

1 red and 1 green
pepper, roasted
(see Tip page 112)

1 tomato

Salt and pepper

Drop of Tabasco®

1. First, prepare the marinated chicken: Thinly slice and lightly salt the chicken breasts. Put the chicken into a zipper freezer bag.

2. Make the marinade: Add the avocado, garlic, peeled and chopped onion, lime and pineapple juices, peppers, and tomato to a blender. Blend for 2 minutes or until smooth. Season to taste with salt, pepper, and Tabasco®.

3. Pour the marinade over the chicken and seal the freezer bag. Massage the meat to coat thoroughly and refrigerate for at least 1 hour.

4. Meanwhile, prepare the corn husks: Bring a large pot of water to a boil; then remove the pot from the heat and drop in the corn husks. Leave them for 30 minutes to soften and then drain and set aside.

5. Prepare the corn dough: Place the lard in the bowl of a stand mixer equipped with a paddle attachment or in a mixing bowl and beat vigorously for 2 minutes until smooth and glossy. Add the salt and stir it in with a silicone spatula. Stir in half the masa harina and baking powder to fully combine; then add the other half and stir until you have a dry dough. While stirring, gradually add the stock until the corn dough forms a smooth ball. Set the dough in a mixing bowl, cover with a damp cloth, and let rest for 15 minutes.

CORN DOUGH
¾ cup lard

Pinch of salt

2 cups masa
harina corn flour, divided

2 teaspoons baking powder

1¼ cups Chicken Stock
(see Tip on page 82)

EQUIPMENT
Blender

Stand mixer with
paddle attachment

Steamer basket

6. Take the marinated chicken strips out of the refrigerator. Pour a drizzle of olive oil into a frying pan and sauté the chicken for 5 minutes over medium heat.

7. Make the tamales: Lay out the corn husks and spread them with a little corn dough, then spoon a little meat along the center of the dough. Use the husks to fold the dough around the meat. Place the tamales in the steamer basket.

8. Steam your tamales for 1 hour 30 minutes and then set them on a plate. Let rest for 20 minutes before serving.

VEGGIE PIZZA

BROCCOLI AND GOAT CHEESE PIZZA

DIFFICULTY:

PREP TIME:
30 minutes

RESTING TIME:
12 hours

COOK TIME:
15 minutes

INGREDIENTS
YIELD: 4 SERVINGS
PIZZA DOUGH
½ cup water at room
temperature

¾ teaspoon active
dry yeast

1 teaspoon olive oil, plus
more for greasing

1¼ cups flour

½ teaspoon table salt

Broccoli pizza is a specialty at the local pizza place where Riley and her family eat after moving to San Francisco from Minnesota. Try this recipe, and you'll see that this unusual pizza can actually be fun and delicious!

1. The night before, make the pizza dough: Pour the water, yeast, and oil into a mixing bowl. Use a whisk or a fork to stir the mixture vigorously; then let it rest for 10 minutes.

2. In a separate mixing bowl, stir together the flour and salt and then add the mixed wet ingredients. Continue to mix with your fingers for about 5 minutes until the dough forms a ball. Let rest for 12 minutes. Dust your work surface with flour and turn out the dough to knead it for another 3 to 4 minutes. Your pizza dough is almost ready. Oil and then flour a mixing bowl. Set the ball of dough in the bowl and cover it tightly with plastic wrap. Leave the mixing bowl in the refrigerator for at least 12 hours while the dough doubles in volume.

3. The next day, prepare the broccoli: Wash and cut it into florets. Cook the broccoli for 10 minutes in a large pot of salted, boiling water. The florets should be cooked but retain some bite. Drain the broccoli florets and slice them into strips. Set aside.

4. Preheat the oven to 425°F.

TOPPINGS

1 small head broccoli

3½ ounces fresh goat cheese

3½ ounces ricotta cheese

A few sage leaves

A few parsley stems

One 5-ounce ball fresh mozzarella cheese

Olive oil

A few basil leaves for garnishing

Salt and pepper

5. Prepare the sauce base: In a mixing bowl, combine the goat cheese and ricotta. Season with salt and pepper. Finely chop the sage and parsley and then add them to the cheese mixture. Mix well and set aside.

6. Cut the mozzarella into thin slices or small cubes.

7. Next, make the pizza: Take the dough out of the refrigerator. Flour your work surface and hands. Flatten the dough with the palm of your hand and use your fingertips to form a thicker crust around the edge.

8. Place the uncooked pizza crust on a baking sheet and top with the cheese mixture, sliced broccoli, and mozzarella. Drizzle with olive oil and bake for 15 minutes.

TO PLATE: Serve the pizza hot from the oven, sprinkled with a few fresh basil leaves.

Delicious!

JACK-JACK'S COOKIES

CHOCOLATE CHIP COOKIES WITH ALEPPO PEPPER

DIFFICULTY:

PREP TIME:
15 minutes

RESTING TIME:
1 hour 30 minutes
plus 10 minutes

COOK TIME:
15 minutes

INGREDIENTS

YIELD: 16 COOKIES

1⅔ cups flour

4 teaspoons
baking powder

1 teaspoon cornstarch

Pinch of salt

¾ cup salted butter

¾ cup brown sugar

½ cup sugar

1 whole egg plus 1 yolk

¾ cup chocolate chips

¼ teaspoon
Aleppo pepper

The youngest member of the Parr family can be a little explosive—literally. Luckily, it's safe to keep Jack-Jack's favorite chocolate chip cookies on hand at your house!

1. Combine the flour, baking powder, cornstarch, and salt in a mixing bowl.

2. Melt the butter and pour it into a separate mixing bowl. Add the brown and white sugar and stir well before thoroughly beating in the whole egg and egg yolk.

3. Stir together the wet and dry ingredients; then add the chocolate chips and sprinkle with Aleppo pepper. Mix. Refrigerate the cookie dough for at least 1 hour 30 minutes.

4. After the dough has rested, preheat the oven to 350°F. Remove the dough from the refrigerator and form into 16 relatively large balls. Arrange the dough balls on a baking sheet lined with parchment paper, leaving space between them for the cookies to spread as they bake. Bake for 15 to 20 minutes, or until lightly golden brown.

5. Remove the cookies from the oven and cool for 10 minutes on a wire rack before eating.

HERCULADE

CHERRY-BLUEBERRY ENERGY DRINK

Herculade is an energy drink that the young hero guzzles during the film. Mix up a batch the next time you need to go the distance!

DIFFICULTY:

PREP TIME:
10 minutes

INGREDIENTS

YIELD: 4 GLASSES
10½ ounces
pitted cherries

10½ ounces blueberries

1 cup grape juice

¼ cup orange juice

3 tablespoons
Greek yogurt

EQUIPMENT
Blender

1. Making this energy drink couldn't be simpler. First, put the cherries and blueberries in a blender. Add the grape and orange juices and blend on high speed for 30 seconds.

2. Finally, add the Greek yogurt and blend for another 30 seconds.

3. Serve and drink immediately to enjoy the antioxidant benefits of this delicious beverage.

TIPS

LEMONY YOGURT SAUCE

Prep time:
5 minutes

INGREDIENTS
2 cups Greek yogurt

Juice of 1 lemon

10 fresh chives

Salt and pepper

Pour the Greek yogurt into a mixing bowl. Add the lemon juice. Finely chop the chives and stir into the yogurt mixture. Season with salt and pepper. That's it!

ROASTED PEPPERS

Make your own roasted peppers using one of these two simple methods:

IN THE OVEN:
Preheat the oven to 400°F.

Arrange the peppers on a baking sheet lined with parchment paper. Bake for 45 minutes, until the skin of the peppers is black all over.

Remove the peppers from the oven and seal them in a sheet of aluminum foil for 15 minutes; then peel off the skin. Your roasted peppers are ready!

OVER A FLAME:
If you have a gas stove, you can place the peppers where they are directly in contact with the flame and roast until the skin is black all over. Seal the peppers in a sheet of aluminum foil for 15 minutes; then peel off the skin. Your roasted peppers are ready!

HOMEMADE STRAWBERRY SYRUP

Prep time:
10 minutes

INGREDIENTS
YIELD: 1½ CUPS OF SYRUP
9 ounces fresh strawberries

⅔ cup sugar

⅔ cup water

Hull and halve the strawberries.

Blend them with the sugar and water for 1 minute.

Pass the mixture through a fine mesh strainer to obtain a clear syrup.

HAMBURGER BUNS

Prep time: 10 minutes
Resting time: 1 hour
15 minutes
Cook time: 12 minutes

INGREDIENTS
YIELD: 4 BUNS
2½ cups (340 grams)
all-purpose flour

1 packet (¾ ounces)
active dry yeast

1½ teaspoon sugar

¾ cup plus 2 tablespoons
warm milk

Scant ¼ cup butter, chopped

1 egg yolk

Add the flour, yeast, and sugar to a mixing bowl. Stir well and add the warm milk. Knead with your fingers to thoroughly mix.

Place the mixture in the bowl of a stand mixer and beat on a slow setting for 2 to 3 minutes. Add the butter and beat for another 7 minutes, until the dough is smooth and glossy. Cover the dough with a tea towel and let rise for 45 minutes.

Dust your work surface with flour. Punch down the dough to deflate and then separate it into 4 equal pieces. Use the palms of your hands to form each piece into a ball. Cover the balls again and let rise for another 30 minutes.

Preheat the oven to 425°F. Beat the egg yolk and use a pastry brush to coat the balls of dough. Bake the buns for 12 minutes, until golden brown.

SPICY MAYONNAISE

Prep time: 10 minutes

INGREDIENTS
YIELD: 1 BOWL
3 egg yolks

2 teaspoons mustard

Salt and freshly ground
pepper

2½ cups sunflower oil

1 tablespoon sriracha sauce

Juice of ½ lime

Important note: All the ingredients must be at room temperature, or at least at the same temperature, for the emulsion to form.

Add the egg yolks to a mixing bowl. Add the mustard and then salt and pepper to taste. Whisk to form a smooth cream.

Gradually drizzle in the oil, continuing to whisk constantly, until the ingredients form an emulsion. When you have a creamy mayonnaise, add the sriracha and lime juice and whisk briefly to combine. Enjoy your homemade mayonnaise with a touch of heat.

Wonderland

AND OTHER FANTASY WORLDS

HARRYHAUSEN'S CHEF SPECIAL

SALMON AND GRILLED OCTOPUS SUSHI

There is no hotter spot in Monstropolis than Harryhausen's, the sushi restaurant where Mike Wazowski takes his girlfriend Celia on a special date. Impress your guests with a few hand-picked selections from the menu.

DIFFICULTY:

PREP TIME:
20 minutes

RESTING TIME:
50 minutes

COOK TIME:
10 minutes plus 40 minutes

INGREDIENTS

YIELD: 2 SERVINGS

SUSHI RICE
2 cups short-grain
sushi rice

5 tablespoons rice vinegar

3 tablespoons
granulated sugar

1 teaspoon salt

1. First, make the sushi rice: Rinse the dry rice until the water runs clear. Add the rice to a saucepan with 2 cups of water and bring to a boil. Reduce heat to very low to simmer for 12 minutes; then remove pot from heat and set aside for 10 minutes, covered.

2. Meanwhile, add the rice vinegar, sugar, and salt to a small saucepan. Cook over low heat until the salt and sugar dissolve; do not boil. Set aside.

3. Scoop the rice from the pot into a large bowl. Pour the vinegar mixture over the rice and cut it in carefully with a wooden spatula to avoid crushing the grains. At the same time, fan the rice to cool it slightly. Set the finished sushi rice aside under a damp cloth.

4. Next, prepare the octopuses: Drop the tentacle and baby octopuses into a large pot of boiling, salted water for 35 minutes. Drain and place in a freezer bag.

5. Add the teriyaki sauce, oyster sauce, sake, and soy sauce to the bag and seal. Mix and knead the bag to fully coat the octopus with marinade. Let rest for 30 minutes before sautéing.

MARINATED OCTOPUS

1 large octopus tentacle

8 baby octopuses

¼ cup teriyaki sauce

1 teaspoon oyster sauce

1 tablespoon cooking sake

1 tablespoon soy sauce

Olive oil, for cooking

SALMON SUSHI

1 fillet fatty salmon

Prepared wasabi for assembling the sushi

Soy sauce for dipping

6. Heat a frying pan with a drizzle of olive oil over high heat and add the marinated octopus. Sauté for 1 minute on each side and then remove from the pan. Reduce heat to medium and pour the marinade into the pan. Cook the sauce for 2 minutes to reduce and then pour it into a bowl.

7. Finally, thinly slice the salmon. Dip your hands into a bowl of water with a splash of rice vinegar to prevent sticking. Then, take a small ball of sushi rice and form it into a rounded rectangle, about the length of the salmon slices. Dab a little wasabi on the top of the rice ball and lay a slice of salmon over the top.

TO PLATE: Arrange the salmon sushi on a platter with soy sauce for dipping. Serve the baby octopus and tentacle along with the reduced sauce.

Itadakimasu!

KING LOUIE'S FRUIT SALAD

INDIAN-INSPIRED FRUIT PLATTER

DIFFICULTY:

PREP TIME:
15 minutes

RESTING TIME:
30 minutes

INGREDIENTS

YIELD: 4 SERVINGS

1 blood orange

Juice of 2 Valencia
oranges

1 teaspoon agave syrup

1 vanilla bean

1 small pineapple

2 large mangoes

2 bananas

2 apples

2 kiwis

Seeds from
1 pomegranate

When King Louie sings "I Wanna Be Like You" to Mowgli, we learn about his true motives . . . and his love of fruit! This exotic fruit salad will make you want to get up and dance.

1. First, make a flavored juice as dressing for your fruit salad: Zest the blood orange into a bowl. Peel and supreme the orange using a paring knife. Set aside.

2. Pour the orange juice and agave syrup over the zest. Split the vanilla bean in half and scrape out the seeds, adding them along with the pod to the juice mixture. Stir well. Refrigerate the orange juice mixture for 30 minutes to candy the zest.

3. Now, prepare the fruit: Peel the pineapple and cut into large cubes. Peel and pit the mangoes and slice into thick strips. Peel the bananas and cut into rounds. Peel and core the apples and cut into bite-sized pieces. Peel the kiwis and cut into small cubes.

4. Arrange the cut fruit attractively on a dish and sprinkle with pomegranate seeds. Finally, drizzle your vanilla-infused orange juice over the fruit and enjoy!

MAD HATTER'S MUFFINS

BLACKBERRY MINT MUFFINS

DIFFICULTY:

PREP TIME:
20 minutes

COOK TIME:
20 minutes

INGREDIENTS

YIELD: 10 MUFFINS

⅔ cup milk

⅓ cup butter

1 egg

¾ cup sugar

1¼ cup flour

2 teaspoons baking powder

Pinch of salt

8 drops red food coloring

6 drops blue food coloring

A few mint leaves

⅔ cup blackberries

I like to imagine that these quintessentially English treats are just what the Mad Hatter would serve for tea!

1. Preheat the oven to 350°F.

2. Add the milk and butter to a saucepan over medium heat. Melt the butter; then remove the saucepan from the heat.

3. Break the egg into a mixing bowl and add the sugar. Whisk vigorously until frothy. Add the flour, baking powder, and salt.

4. Next, add the milk and butter mixture and stir until the batter is smooth. Mix the red and blue food coloring together in a spoon and add to the batter. Finely chop the mint leaves and stir them in along with the blackberries. Your muffin batter is ready.

5. Divide the batter into 10 lined or greased muffin tins and bake for 20 minutes.

6. Savor these muffins warm, with a pot of Earl Grey tea . . . that is, unless you're late for a very important date!

CROWN OF ARENDELLE

SOFT BUNDT CAKE WITH CHESTNUT CREAM

DIFFICULTY:

PREP TIME:
15 minutes

COOK TIME:
35 minutes

INGREDIENTS

YIELD: 6 SERVINGS

CAKE

¾ cup flour

¾ cup chestnut flour

2 teaspoons baking powder

Pinch of salt

¾ cup butter

4 eggs

½ cup sugar

½ cup brown sugar

12 ounces chestnut cream

3 tablespoons whole milk

⅓ cup toasted hazelnuts

10 candied chestnuts

GLAZE

2 egg whites

1 tablespoon powdered sugar

Juice of ½ lemon

Juice of ½ orange

EQUIPMENT
Bundt pan

After years apart, Anna and Elsa are finally reunited for Elsa's coronation ceremony. This decadent cake graces the banquet table at the coronation ball.

1. Preheat the oven to 350°F. Stir together the flour, chestnut flour, baking powder, and salt in a mixing bowl. Set aside.

2. In a saucepan, melt the butter over low heat and then remove the saucepan from the heat.

3. Separate the egg yolks from the whites. Add the egg yolks to a mixing bowl and vigorously whisk in the sugar and brown sugar until frothy. While whisking, add the chestnut cream, milk, and melted butter. Add the dry ingredients and stir in thoroughly. Beat the egg whites until they form stiff peaks, taking care not to overmix. Use a silicone spatula to fold the egg whites into the batter delicately so as not to deflate them. Your cake batter is ready.

4. Grease the bundt pan, pour in the batter, and bake for 35 minutes.

5. Meanwhile, prepare the orange glaze: Add the egg whites, powdered sugar, lemon juice, and orange juice to a mixing bowl and whisk to make a translucent glaze.

6. When the cake is finished baking, remove it from the pan and let cool on a wire rack. Drizzle the glaze over the cooled cake. Crush the candied chestnuts and the hazelnuts and use them to decorate the cake.

TO PLATE: Serve your guests thick slices of this decadent cake with a scoop of vanilla or rum raisin ice cream.

COOKIE MEDALS

ICED GINGER COOKIES

DIFFICULTY:

PREP TIME:
10 minutes

RESTING TIME:
15 minutes

COOK TIME:
12 minutes

INGREDIENTS

YIELD: ABOUT 12 COOKIES

COOKIES

⅓ cup brown sugar

7 tablespoons unsalted butter, at room temperature

1 egg

2 cups flour

2 teaspoons baking powder

½ teaspoon ground cinnamon

½ teaspoon ground ginger

½ teaspoon pumpkin pie spice

1⅔ cups (200 g) powdered sugar

Pamper your own hero by baking the cookie medal that Princess Vanellope gives to Ralph!

1. Add the brown sugar and butter to a mixing bowl and stir with a spatula until smooth. Add the whole egg while stirring vigorously.

2. Add the flour, baking powder, cinnamon, ginger, pumpkin pie spice, and powdered sugar. Knead with your hands to form a ball of dough. Wrap the dough with plastic wrap and refrigerate for 15 minutes.

3. Preheat the oven to 350°F.

4. Dust your work surface with flour, remove the dough from the refrigerator, and roll it out to a thickness of ¼ inch. Use a heart-shaped cookie cutter to cut out your cookies; then space them out on a baking sheet lined with parchment paper. Bake for 10 to 12 minutes.

5. Meanwhile, prepare the royal icing you will use to decorate your cookies: Add the egg white and powdered sugar to a mixing bowl. Stir together and then thin with the lemon juice to desired consistency.

ROYAL ICING

1 egg white

1¼ cups sifted
powdered sugar

Juice of 1 lemon

Blue food coloring

6. Divide the icing into two bowls and add a drop of blue food coloring to one. Put the icing into two piping bags and set aside.

7. Remove the cookies from the oven when ready and let them cool to room temperature. Pipe white icing around the edge of each heart, fill with blue, and then write *You're my hero* in white icing. That's it!

B.E.N. SPECIAL

NO-BAKE OREO® CHEESECAKE

DIFFICULTY: ✖✖

PREP TIME:
30 minutes

RESTING TIME:
5 hours

INGREDIENTS

YIELD: 6 SERVINGS

20 ounces Oreo® cookies

7 tablespoons butter

5 ounces mascarpone,
very cold

⅔ cup whipping cream,
very cold

5 ounces cream cheese,
very cold

1 teaspoon vanilla extract

5 tablespoons sugar

B.E.N. is a clumsy, eccentric robot who works at the inn owned by Jim Hawkins's mother. In the film, he walks out of the kitchen holding several slices of layer cake. Here is the recipe.

1. Put a mixing bowl or the bowl of your stand mixer into the freezer.

2. First, prepare the Oreo® cookies: Scrape the cream from each cookie into a mixing bowl. Set aside in the refrigerator. Put the chocolate biscuits into a separate mixing bowl and crush them. Set aside.

3. In a saucepan, melt the butter. Pour the melted butter over the crushed biscuits and stir well to form a cookie crumb crust mixture.

4. On a piece of parchment paper, divide the crust mixture into 3 portions and flatten 2 of them so that they fit into the removable bottom of a springform pan. Refrigerate the two Oreo® cookie crusts for 30 minutes.

5. Press the remaining portion of crust mixture into the bottom of your springform pan in a dense, even layer. Refrigerate the pan with the crust for 30 minutes.

6. Take the mixing bowl out of your freezer. Pour in the mascarpone, whipping cream, cream cheese, and Oreo® cream filling. Add the vanilla extract and beat vigorously for 1 minute. While continuing to beat, gradually pour in the sugar and beat for another 2 minutes, or until the cream forms stiff peaks.

7. Take the springform pan back out of the refrigerator. Line the sides with an acetate sheet. Pour half of the vanilla whipped cream into the springform pan. Carefully place the first Oreo® cookie crust round on top. Spread the remaining whipped cream over it in an even layer.

8. Cover with the final Oreo® cookie crust. Press gently with your fingertips and place the cheesecake in the refrigerator for at least 4 hours 30 minutes before serving.

HONEY CAKE

MULTI-FLOWER HONEY CAKE

DIFFICULTY:

PREP TIME:
15 minutes

COOK TIME:
35 minutes

INGREDIENTS

YIELD: 6 SERVINGS
CAKE

4 eggs

1 cup sugar

Pinch of salt

1⅔ cups flour

⅔ cup unsalted butter,
melted and cooled

2 teaspoons
baking powder

1 teaspoon ground
ginger

3 tablespoons
multi-flower honey

HONEY CREAM
10½ ounces
mascarpone

2 tablespoons
liquid honey

3½ ounces candied
fruit for decorating

Edible flowers
for decorating

EQUIPMENT
Hand mixer

Everyone knows how much Pooh loves honey. In The Many Adventures of Winnie the Pooh, *Pooh and Piglet share a delicious honey cake. Maybe it's time for a little something at your house, too?*

1. Preheat the oven to 350°F.

2. Grease a round cake pan and then prepare the cake batter. Separate the egg yolks and whites into two mixing bowls. Add the pinch of salt to the egg whites and beat with a hand mixer until they form stiff peaks.

3. In the other bowl, add the sugar to the egg yolks. Whisk vigorously until the mixture becomes frothy and lighter in color. While whisking, add the flour, melted butter, baking powder, ginger, honey, and beaten egg whites. The goal is to create a smooth, airy batter. Pour the batter into the cake pan and bake for 35 minutes.

4. While the cake is baking, make the honey cream. Add the mascarpone to a mixing bowl. Using a whisk or hand mixer, whip the mascarpone while gradually drizzling in the honey.

5. When it has finished baking, gently turn the cake out of the pan.

TO PLATE: Spread a thick layer of honeyed mascarpone cream over the cake. Garnish with candied fruit and edible flowers.

HOPPS CAKE

CARROT CAKE

As you may have noticed from watching Zootopia, the Hopps are obsessed with all things carrot. I designed this spiced carrot cake for Judy's family.

DIFFICULTY:

PREP TIME:
20 minutes

35 minutes

RESTING TIME:
45 minutes

INGREDIENTS
YIELD: 4 SERVINGS

CAKE
2 cups cake flour

2 teaspoons cinnamon

1 teaspoon ground ginger

4 teaspoons baking powder

Pinch of salt

4 eggs

½ cup granulated sugar

¼ cup brown sugar

1 tablespoon dark rum

⅔ cup vegetable oil

14 ounces carrots, finely grated

¼ cup blanched hazelnuts

¼ cup blanched almonds

MASCARPONE
FROSTING
4 ounces mascarpone
(or cream cheese)

¼ cup butter at room temperature

1 tablespoon chestnut cream

⅔ cup powdered sugar

1. Preheat the oven to 350°F.

2. Make the cake batter: Stir together the flour, cinnamon, ginger, baking powder, and salt in a large mixing bowl.

3. Break the eggs into a separate mixing bowl, add the granulated and brown sugars and rum and whisk vigorously until smooth. Gradually stir in the vegetable oil. Add the dry ingredients in 3 portions, stirring between each addition. Gradually stir in the grated carrots. Crush the nuts and add them to the batter. Your cake batter is ready.

4. Grease a round cake pan or a loaf pan and line the sides with a strip of parchment paper. Pour the batter into the pan and bake for 35 minutes.

5. Check for doneness (a knife inserted into the middle should come out clean). Remove the cake from the oven and let cool.

6. Meanwhile, prepare the mascarpone and chestnut frosting: Add the mascarpone (or cream cheese) to a mixing bowl. Add the butter and chestnut cream and use a hand mixer to beat on high speed for 1 minute, until smooth.

7. Reduce the mixer speed to low and beat in the powdered sugar until the frosting is glossy. Remove the cooled cake from the pan. Spread a thick layer of frosting over it and refrigerate for at least 45 minutes before serving.

HERBARIUM

Dill

A highly fragrant plant with an aroma reminiscent of fennel and anise. Used mainly to flavor fish.

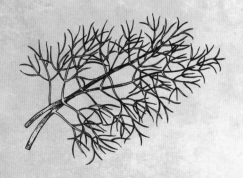

Basil

A fragrant, flavorful plant, its leaves are often used fresh, when their flavor is most pronounced.

Basil is frequently used in Italian and Mediterranean cooking.

Chives

Chives are used raw, usually finely chopped. Like other tender herbs, they are most flavorful when used fresh. Chives add flavor to salads and sauces as well as dishes such as traditional French omelets.

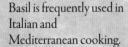

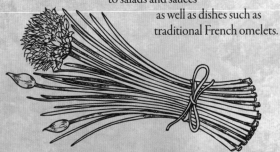

Cilantro

This pungent plant is easily recognizable by the shape of its leaves.

Its slightly spicy flavor is highly prized in Asian, Middle Eastern, and South American cuisine.

Use it in soups and stocks or with grilled meat.

Tarragon

This fragrant, herbaceous plant is used to flavor soups, simple dishes, and meats. It is best fresh, never dried. Tarragon lends its flavor to several classic French sauces, including béarnaise and ravigote.

Bay leaves

There are different types of laurel trees, but the one used in cooking is the bay laurel.

This aromatic plant is native to the Mediterranean region.

Dried, it is one of the herbs included in a bouquet garnish. Bay leaves are used mainly to flavor sauces and stocks.

MINT

An aromatic plant used not only in cooking, but also in cocktails and various steeped and infused liquids. There are many varieties of and uses for mint. In the kitchen, it adds a refreshing note to raw vegetables, sauces, and salads as well as desserts, fruit salads, creams, and mousses.

PARSLEY

Both curly and flat-leaf parsley are widely used in French cooking, particularly for dishes from the south of France. It features alongside garlic in classic compound butter, and it is also used to season sauces, salads, and meats.

OREGANO

Oregano is part of any Herbes de Provence blend. This aromatic plant is most often used dried. Mediterranean and Italian recipes often add oregano to flavor sauces.

ROSEMARY

Rosemary is one of the herbs in a traditional Herbes de Provence blend, along with sage, thyme, tarragon, and oregano.

Its flavor is subtle yet present. Its resinous scent is similar to incense, and it is equally good in sweet and savory dishes.

SAGE

A pungent herb with a slightly bitter flavor. It pairs beautifully with white meats, such as veal.

THYME

Thyme is widely found in Mediterranean dishes and can be used fresh or dried. It adds a hint of bitterness and a slightly earthy flavor.

It is delicious in combination with other herbs, such as rosemary, and is one of the ingredients in a bouquet garnish.

INDEX

Imperial Jiaozi 28
Kay's Banquet 68

CINNAMON
Cookie Medals 126
Hopps Cake 134
Kanine Krunchies 79
Kay's Banquet 68

CLOVES
Gumbo Stock 81

COMTÉ CHEESE
Royal Soufflé 27

CORN HUSKS, DRIED
Abuelita's Tamales 100

CORN ON THE COB
New World Corn 18

CORNSTARCH
Royal Soufflé 27
Tournament Fruit Pie 76
Tropical Kalua Pig 33

CREAM CHEESE
B.E.N. Special 130
Hopps Cake 87

CUMIN
Kay's Banquet 68
Pizza Planet Super Nova Burger 97
Prince Ali's Kebabs 99

D

DUCK BREAST, SMOKED
New World Corn 18

E

EGGPLANT
Geppetto's Grilled Fish 64
Nostalgic Ratatouille 60
Oven Fries 83

EGGPLANT, GRAFFITI
Nostalgic Ratatouille 60

EGGS
A Pie for Grumpy 42
Bear Cub Buns 34
Breakfast Congee 14
Cheese Crackers 80
Cookie Medals 126
Crown of Arendelle 124
Date Night Dinner 92
Honey Cake 12
Hopps Cake 134
Imperial Jiaozi 28
Jack-Jack's Cookies 108
Kanine Krunchies 79
Kronk's Spinach Puffs 87
Mad Hatter's Muffins 123
Modern Fairy Cake 36
Mrs. Judson's Crumpets 51
Pizza Planet Super Nova Burger 97
Quasimodo's Croissants 52
Royal Soufflé 27
Spicy Mayonnaise 113
Sugar Mill Beignets 45
Sweet Almond Dough 81
Tournament Fruit Pie 76

F

FISH, WHOLE
Geppetto's Grilled Fish 64

FLOWERS, EDIBLE
Honey Cake 12

FOOD COLORING, BLUE
Cookie Medals 126
Mad Hatter's Muffins 123
Modern Fairy Cake 36

FOOD COLORING, RED
Ariel's Milkshake 41
Mad Hatter's Muffins 123

G

GARLIC
Abuelita's Tamales 100
Aunt Cass's Wings 88
Breakfast Congee 14
Chicken or Turkey Stock 82

Date Night Dinner 92
Geppetto's Grilled Fish 64
Gumbo Stock 81
Imperial Jiaozi 28
Kay's Banquet 68
Kronk's Spinach Puffs 87
Little John's Spicy Stew 72
Nostalgic Ratatouille 60
Prince Ali's Kebabs 99
Tiana's Gumbo 30

GINGER
Aunt Cass's Wings 88
Breakfast Congee 14
Cookie Medals 126
Honey Cake 12
Hopps Cake 134
Imperial Jiaozi 28
Kanine Krunchies 79
Kay's Banquet 68
Little John's Spicy Stew 72

GOAT CHEESE, FRESH
Veggie Pizza 104

GREEK YOGURT
Herculade 110
Lemony Yogurt Sauce 112

GYOZA WRAPPERS
Imperial Jiaozi 28

H

HAZELNUTS
Crown of Arendelle 124
Date Night Dinner 92
Hopps Cake 134
Mother Gothel's Soup 21
Stroke of Midnight Soup 22

HONEY
Honey Cake 12
Kay's Banquet 68

I

ICE CREAM, PISTACHIO
Ariel's Milkshake 41

ICE CREAM, VANILLA
Ariel's Milkshake 41

J

JERUSALEM ARTICHOKES
Crème de la Crème à la Edgar 56

JUICE, GRAPE
Herculade 110

JUICE, ORANGE
Herculade 110

JUICE, PINEAPPLE
Abuelita's Tamales 100
Tropical Kalua Pig 33

JUNIPER BERRIES
Chicken or Turkey Stock 82

K

KETCHUP
Tropical Kalua Pig 33

KIWI
King Louie's Fruit Salad 120

L

LAMB (GROUND)
Prince Ali's Kebabs 99

LARD
Abuelita's Tamales 100

LEEK, ENTIRE
Vegetable Stock 80

LEEK, WHITE PART
Remy's Soup 58
Stroke of Midnight Soup 22

LEMON
Cookie Medals 126
Crown of Arendelle 124
Geppetto's Grilled Fish 64
Lemony Yogurt Sauce 112

LEMONGRASS
Breakfast Congee 14

LIME
Abuelita's Tamales 100

Spicy Mayonnaise 113
Tropical Kalua Pig 33

LIQUID SMOKE
Tropical Kalua Pig 33

M

MANGO
King Louie's Fruit Salad 120

MAPLE SYRUP
New World Corn 18

MARASCHINO CHERRIES
Bear Cub Buns 34

MASA HARINA
Abuelita's Tamales 100

MASCARPONE
Ariel's Milkshake 41
B.E.N. Special 130
Honey Cake 12
Hopps Cake 134
Modern Fairy Cake 36

MILK, WHOLE
Ariel's Milkshake 41
Crown of Arendelle 124
Sugar Mill Beignets 45

MINT
Date Night Dinner 92
Mad Hatter's Muffins 123

MOZZARELLA
Veggie Pizza 105

MUSTARD
Spicy Mayonnaise 113

N

NUTMEG
Crème de la Crème à la Edgar 56
Mother Gothel's Soup 21
Royal Soufflé 27

O

OCTOPUS
Harryhausen's Chef Special 116

OKRA
Geppetto's Grilled Fish 64

Tiana's Gumbo 30

OLIVES, GREEN
Geppetto's Grilled Fish 64

ONION POWDER
Aunt Cass's Wings 88
Date Night Dinner 92

ONIONS
Abuelita's Tamales 100
Crème de la Crème à la Edgar 56
Date Night Dinner 92
Geppetto's Grilled Fish 64
Gumbo Stock 81
Kay's Banquet 68
Little John's Spicy Stew 72
Nostalgic Ratatouille 60
Prince Ali's Kebabs 99
Remy's Soup 58
Stroke of Midnight Soup 22
Vegetable Stock 80

ONIONS, RED
Prince Ali's Kebabs 99

ONIONS, SPRING
Prince Ali's Kebabs 99

ONIONS, YELLOW
Tiana's Gumbo 30

ORANGES
Bear Cub Buns 34
Crown of Arendelle 124
King Louie's Fruit Salad 120

ORANGES, BLOOD
King Louie's Fruit Salad 120

OREGANO, DRIED
Date Night Dinner 92
Nostalgic Ratatouille 60

OREO
B.E.N. Special 130

OYSTER SAUCE
Harryhausen's Chef Special 116

P

PAPRIKA
Aunt Cass's Wings 88

Pizza Planet Super Nova Burger 97

PARSLEY
Breakfast Congee 14
Veggie Pizza 104

PARSLEY, FLAT-LEAF
Compound Butter 80
Gumbo Stock 81
Kay's Banquet 68
Little John's Spicy Stew 72
Mother Gothel's Soup 21
Nostalgic Ratatouille 60
Remy's Soup 58
Stroke of Midnight Soup 22
Tiana's Gumbo 30

PARSNIPS
Deep Fryer Fries 83
Mother Gothel's Soup 21

PEANUTS (UNSALTED)
Breakfast Congee 14

PEAS
Little John's Spicy Stew 72

PEPPER, GREEN
Geppetto's Grilled Fish 64
Tiana's Gumbo 30

PEPPER, RED
Geppetto's Grilled Fish 64
Nostalgic Ratatouille 60
Pizza Planet Super Nova Burger 97
Prince Ali's Kebabs 99
Tiana's Gumbo 30

PINEAPPLE
King Louie's Fruit Salad 120
Tropical Kalua Pig 33

PLUMS
A Pie for Grumpy 42

POMEGRANATE
King Louie's Fruit Salad 120

PORK, GROUND
Imperial Jiaozi 28

PORK SHOULDER
Tropical Kalua Pig 33

POTATOES
Aunt Cass's Wings 88
Crème de la Crème à la Edgar 56
Deep Fryer Fries 83
Geppetto's Grilled Fish 64
Little John's Spicy Stew 72
Mother Gothel's Soup 21
Oven Fries 83
Remy's Soup 58
Stroke of Midnight Soup 22

POTATOES, BABY
Kay's Banquet 68

PUFF PASTRY
Kronk's Spinach Puffs 87

PUMPKIN
Stroke of Midnight Soup 22

PUMPKIN PIE SPICE
Cookie Medals 126

R

RICE
Tropical Kalua Pig 33

RICE, SHORT-GRAIN
Breakfast Congee 14

RICE, 4USHI
Harryhausen's Chef Special 116

RICOTTA
Veggie Pizza 104
Kronk's Spinach Puffs 87

ROQUEFORT
Cheese Crackers 80

ROSEMARY
Chicken or Turkey Stock 82
Date Night Dinner 92
Geppetto's Grilled Fish 64
Nostalgic Ratatouille 60

RUM, DARK
Hopps Cake 134

S

SAGE
Geppetto's Grilled Fish 64
Veggie Pizza 104

SAKE, COOKING
Aunt Cass's Wings 88
Harryhausen's Chef Special 116
Tropical Kalua Pig 33

SALMON, FILLET
Harryhausen's Chef Special 116

SALT, ALAEA RED
Tropical Kalua Pig 33

SAUSAGE, ITALIAN
Date Night Dinner 92

SAUSAGE, SMOKED
Tiana's Gumbo 30

SHALLOTS
Chicken or Turkey Stock 82
Date Night Dinner 92
Kronk's Spinach Puffs 87
Mother Gothel's Soup 21
Pizza Planet Super
Nova Burger 97
Tiana's Gumbo 30
Vegetable Stock 80

SHRIMP
Imperial Jiaozi 28
Tiana's Gumbo 30

SHRIMP SHELLS
Gumbo Stock 81

SOY SAUCE
Aunt Cass's Wings 88
Harryhausen's Chef Special 116
Tropical Kalua Pig 33

SPAGHETTI
Date Night Dinner 92

SPINACH, FRESH
Kronk's Spinach Puffs 87

SPIRULINA POWDER
Ariel's Milkshake 41

SQUASH, WINTER
Deep Fryer Fries 83

SRIRACHA
Spicy Mayonnaise 113

STAR ANISE
Vegetable Stock   80

STILTON
Mrs. Judson's Crumpets   51

STRAWBERRIES
Ariel's Milkshake   41
Homemade Strawberry Syrup 112

SUMAC
Prince Ali's Kebabs   99

SWEET POTATOES
Oven Fries   83
Tiana's Gumbo   30

T

TEA, LOOSE LEAF JASMINE
Modern Fairy Cake   36

TENTACLE, OCTOPUS
Harryhausen's Chef Special   116

TERIYAKI SAUCE
Harryhausen's Chef Special   116

THAI BASIL
Imperial Jiaozi   28

THYME
Geppetto's Grilled Fish   64
Gumbo Stock   81

THYME, DRIED
Date Night Dinner   92
Nostalgic Ratatouille   60
Oven Fries   83

TOMATOES
Abuelita's Tamales   100
Nostalgic Ratatouille   60
Prince Ali's Kebabs   99

TOMATOES, SUN-DRIED
Kronk's Spinach Puffs   87

TOMATO PASTE
Aunt Cass's Wings   88
Little John's Spicy Stew   72

TOMATO SAUCE
Date Night Dinner   92

TURKEY
Kay's Banquet   68

TURMERIC
Kay's Banquet   68

V

VANILLA BEAN
A Pie for Grumpy   42
King Louie's Fruit Salad   120

VANILLA EXTRACT
B.E.N Special   130
Bear Cub Buns   30
Kanine Krunchies   79
Modern Fairy Cake   36

VEAL (GROUND)
Pizza Planet Super
Nova Burger   97

VINEGAR, RICE
Aunt Cass's Wings   88
Harryhausen's Chef Special   116
Tropical Kalua Pig   33

W

WASABI
Harryhausen's Chef Special   116

WHITE BUTTON MUSHROOMS
Breakfast Congee   14

WINE, WHITE
Vegetable Stock   80

Z

ZUCCHINI, GREEN
Geppetto's Grilled Fish   64
Nostalgic Ratatouille   60
Oven Fries   83

ZUCCHINI, YELLOW
Nostalgic Ratatouille   60

I want to thank everyone who contributed to this very unique book.

Special thanks to my wife, Bérengère, whose talent and guidance have been making me a better man and a better cook since I started my very first book. To my son, Henri, I can't wait to watch all these animated films and cook these recipes with you!

Thank you to my family: to my mother and father for teaching and loving me, and sharing their passion for the good things in life and for doing things right. And to my little sister, for always giving honest—and spot-on!—advice. I love you.

Thank you to my friends Adrien, Satoru, Anna, and Julien, who I don't see as often as I'd like. And Romane, I miss all the time we spent watching and collecting these films.

Thank you to my mentors and friends, Olivier and Marcus, old hands at this pop culture business who have done so much for me these past few years. A special thank you to Maxime—colleague, managing editor, and new acquaintance this year in 2019—for offering wise counsel that has helped me grow as a designer.

Finally, thank you to Soizic and Nicolas, whose enthusiasm and tireless efforts have brought my dream worlds, and my recipes, to life.

Thank you to Catherine, Antoine, and Anne from Hachette Heroes for their faith in me these past years. And thank you also to them and to Sophie at Disney France for entrusting me with the incredible task of creating such a magical cookbook.

Thank you to everyone at Hachette Heroes who will put this cookbook into your hands and make sure it gets the attention it deserves.

Thibaud Villanova

INSIGHT EDITIONS

PO Box 3088
San Rafael, CA 94912
www.insighteditions.com

Find us on Facebook: www.facebook.com/
InsightEditions
Follow us on Twitter: @insighteditions

The Hundred and One Dalmatians is a novel by Dodie Smith published by Viking Press.

The Aristocats is based on a story by Tom Rowe.

The Great Mouse Detective is based on the book series by the same name by Eve Titus and Paul Galdone.

The characters in *Winnie the Pooh* are based on the stories by A. A. Milne and E. H. Shepard.

The story for *The Princess and the Frog*, copyright © 2009 Disney, is loosely based on *The Frog Princess* by E. D. Baker copyright © 2003, published by Bloomsbury Publishing.

Photo credits: Shutterstock (stockphoto mania, r.classen, Tendo, Vectorchoice, Julietphotography, lavendertime)

© 2019, Hachette Livre (Hachette Pratique).

58 Rue Jean Bleuzen – 92178 Vanves Cedex France

The publisher is committed to using paper made of natural, renewable, recyclable fibers manufactured from wood grown in sustainably managed forests.
Furthermore, the publisher requires its paper suppliers to comply with a recognized environmental certification program.

Managing Editor: Catherine Saunier-Talec
Project Director: Antoine Béon
Project Manager: Anne Vallet
Layout: Bérengère Demoncy
Proofreading: Fabienne Vaslet
Printing: Anne-Laure Soyez

Legal deposit: October 2019
38-3761-8/01
ISBN: 978-1-64722-154-6
Printed in China by Toppan Leefung
10 9 8 7 6 5 4 3

www.hachette-heroes.com
facebook.com/hachetteheroes

Join us on YouTube to continue the adventure:
www.youtube.com/gastronogeek

www.facebook.com/gastronogeek www.twitter.com/gastronogeek www.instagram.com/gastronogeek
www.gastronogeek.com